AROUND T[illegible]

Around the World in Cycle Clips

JOHN HANSON

with best wishes,
John Hanson
31st May 1990.

KINGSWAY PUBLICATIONS
EASTBOURNE

First published 1990

The front cover shows John Hanson in the East of India.

British Library Cataloguing in Publication Data

Hanson, John
Around the world in cycle clips.
1. Journeys around the world by bicycles
I. Title
910.41

ISBN 0–86065–774–4

All royalties from the sale of this book will go to Tear Fund.

Printed in Great Britain for
KINGSWAY PUBLICATIONS LTD
1 St Anne's Road, Eastbourne, E Sussex BN21 3UN by
Richard Clay Ltd, Bungay, Suffolk
Typeset by J&L Composition Ltd, Filey, N Yorkshire

Contents

Foreword
by
David Adeney
Executive Director, Tear Fund

John Hanson's fascinating account of his round-the-world cycle trip with John Rodgers is a challenge to all of us to get on our bikes! Few of us, however, even if we took up that challenge, would manage anywhere near the 13,000 miles they notched up in the course of this amazing dream come true.

Such was the magnitude of their task that when they first approached Tear Fund with the idea of cycling roung the world to raise funds for our refugee work in Thailand, it was difficult to believe that they could generate the funds to make a start, let alone carry it off. But not only did they succeed in raising £6,000 to finance the trip, they returned to Dungannon a year after they left having visited sixteen countries and accumulated sufficient experiences to provide a rich store of anecdotes to last a lifetime.

The descriptions John Hanson gives of their travels come across with the freshness of a first impression and are enhanced by his unusual vantage point — the saddle. Where most people would make such journeys by more conventional means of transport, he and his partner chose the hard way, in more senses than one!

As someone who has worked in some of the countries they visited, I felt very much at home when John described their experiences in Pakistan. The Christmas dinner they enjoyed in Rahim Yar Khan consisting of rice and curried goat brought back happy memories. In India, too, I felt for them as they tackled the long haul down the east coast from Calcutta to Madras, rising well before dawn to avoid the heat of the day.

Their 368-day circumnavigation of the world had many moments of danger and distress: armed bandits in Thailand, grizzly bears in Canada, reckless drivers in many countries, mechanical damage to the bikes, bouts of sickness and diarrhoea. But they were not deterred by these and other difficulties; this is a story of hope in adversity and patient endurance.

The book is no mere travelogue, however. The Christian motivation behind this remarkable journey keeps coming through. One of the many incidents I found intensely moving was the night they spent in a Christian village in Pakistan. The man with whom they stayed called the men of the village together while they explained as best they could the purpose of their trip. When they had finished they had the greatest difficulty in dissuading the desperately poor villagers from giving them money to pass on to the refugees they were hoping to visit in Thailand.

The direct result of their round-the-world cycle ride was the raising of more than £54,000 for Tear Fund's ministry there. But that was only the tip of the iceberg. The effect on the two cyclists was profound — and on the many people they met on the road. The fact that more than half the money they raised came after they returned to Northern Ireland, as a result of numerous meetings at which they spoke of their experiences, indicates the scale of the impact they made on their own community.

And now, through the medium of this book, many more people will hear about this cycling marathon with a difference. It will inspire, challenge and amuse all who read it.

David Adeney

Acknowledgements

I would like to thank the following people:

— John for coming with me, putting up with me, and sticking with me through thick and thin;

— the committee of the Third World Cycle Expedition, David Acheson, Fred Doyle, Deirdre Evans, Ivan Gowdy, Alice Hanson, Pam Kirkwood, Will McKee, Andrew Rodgers, Helen Rodgers, Dorothy Ross and May Walker for their wise counsel and their sheer hard work;

— all our supporters for encouraging us with their pounds, prayers and perspiration;

— all those neighbours, rich or poor, who helped us on our way round the world;

— Anne Strain of the Tear Fund office in Belfast for being the catalyst behind the book: many people thought the story should be written down, but she got me started;

— Simon Fox for prising more information out of the recesses of my mind, for rearranging sentences, paragraphs and chapters, increasing my vocabulary and pulling the whole thing together;

Above all I thank God for guidance and protection each and every day, and for giving us this trip of a lifetime.

As it has not been possible to contact all contributors to conversations in the book to gain their approval and permission to use their names and words they said, a few names have been changed.

1
The Idea Is Born

It was dark. I could hear noises above me. Were they real or was I dreaming? Small fragments of debris were falling from the roof on to my face. There was snoring near my feet — whether it was human or animal, I couldn't tell. Then someone on my left coughed and stirred. 'That was definitely human,' I thought, drifting between sleep and consciousness.

I moved my tired legs to a more comfortable position on the mattress and pulled my blanket over my face to keep the falling dust and dirt out of my eyes. There were more noises above me. 'What was that?' I wondered drowsily. There were the noises again. Then there was a frantic flapping. Startled, I pulled the blanket off my face, which was then showered with yet more debris. A hen had just flown off the roof. Silence reigned, but not for long.

There were footsteps outside. Someone was whistling in the distance. Dawn was breaking, and my mind was beginning to clear. But then my chain of thought was suddenly interrupted by an enormous animal roar inside the room. In a flash the man on the bed to my left jumped up shouting, '*Jao! Jao!*' and chased the beast out of the door. I sat up and observed that the animal making its speedy exit was a buffalo calf! The man who was chasing it was dressed from head to foot in baggy white clothes. He didn't return.

Now half awake, I peered through a window and could see small houses made of mud and thatch. People were walking past, hurrying off to work in the fields. Women wearing brightly coloured saris were squatting on the ground preparing breakfast. Buffaloes lay around the village square lazily chewing the cud. Some children were milking goats. A camel taking large but silent steps ambled past, holding his head high in a very dignified manner.

I was in a room just large enough to take three single beds. The walls were thick, grey and made of mud, while the roof was comprised of sticks, thatch and more mud. The clay floor was covered with straw. On one of the beds lay my travelling companion, John Rodgers. Propped against the wall near John's bed were our two sophisticated ten-speed touring bicycles, heavily laden with pregnant panniers.

No, this was no dream, I concluded as I finally became fully awake. This was real. Three months earlier we had left our homes in Northern Ireland to cycle around the world. We had just spent the night in a Pakistani village.

* * *

I have always been a keen traveller. Geography was my best subject at school. Often I would sit and read of faraway places and wonder what it would be like to be there. I wondered what the Alps were like and wanted to see those romantic little Swiss houses. And did Venice really have canals instead of streets? What would it be like to visit Paris, Munich, Tangier? I wondered and I went. I travelled extensively in the British Isles, but my first big trip was to Scandinavia. Another time, I spent a month travelling on the great railways of Europe, living on a shoestring. Travel was in my blood. I was born to it.

As a child, I would often spend hours poring over my atlas, fascinated by the pictures of distant, exotic lands, intrigued by the funny looking clothes on the equally funny looking people, captivated by the pictures of jungles, mountains and deserts. But as I got older, I came to realise that going around the world was expensive. Europe, on the other hand, was comparatively cheap to see, with bargain-priced tickets for people under the age of twenty-six. One could also keep costs down by sleeping in a tent or youth hostels and by buying one's food from supermarkets. This sort of travelling didn't cost me much more than living at home. And besides, I felt that after a hard year's work, I deserved a break in the summer.

I had a conscience about the cost of my travels because I was a Christian. I believed that everything I owned and even my very person in reality belonged to God, and so I was answerable to him as to how I lived and how I spent my money.

Both my parents were committed Christians, and throughout my childhood I went to Sunday school and we prayed together and went to church as a family. But as I grew older, I began to understand that just being brought up in a Christian family didn't automatically make me a Christian, and that young as I was, I needed to personally commit my life to Christ. So at the tender age of twelve, in a very simple way at the side of my bed, I confessed my sinfulness to God and asked Jesus to come into my life as my Saviour to forgive me, as my Lord to control me and as my Friend to be with me. It was as if a great weight had been lifted off my shoulders. I felt secure and safe, and knew that I really was part of God's family.

After I became a Christian, my life and all that was me was no longer my own, but God's. From then on, I could not live for myself but only for God, and must allow God to live through me. I began to read the Bible, which is like a manual for Christian living, written by the Manufacturer himself. At first, though, I couldn't quite see the wood for the trees. The Bible, God's word, makes profound statements about many things, and different groups of Christians emphasise different aspects of its message. What, I wondered, were the priorities of the Christian life according to the Bible? If only I could get these sorted out, the less important issues would then take their rightful places.

So I began to search the Bible, and soon I found my answer: 'Seek first his [God's] kingdom and his righteousness' (Mt 6:33); 'Love the Lord your God with all your heart and with all your soul and with all your strength and with all your mind' and 'Love your neighbour as yourself' (Lk 10:27). These were the most important principles of Christian living. So then I started grappling with the practical implications of putting God first in my life and others on an equal footing with myself.

By the time I was seventeen years old, my thoughts were naturally turning towards the future and what God wanted me to do with my life. One evening I was sitting in my father's car discussing this with my friend Raymond.

'God knows everything, and he knows everything about you,' Raymond reminded me. 'So he knows what's best for you, and he has a plan for your life. If you give the whole of yourself to him, he'll guide you so that you follow that plan.'

'Yes, I really want to do that — I really want to give the whole of myself to God,' I affirmed. 'He sent his only Son to die for me, so now I want to live completely for him and to follow the plan he's mapped out for me. But what bothers me is, how do I find out what that plan is?'

'Do you need to know the whole plan?' asked

Raymond. 'You don't need to know what lies ten steps ahead, or even two steps ahead, for that matter. If you're prepared to do whatever God wants you to do, he'll guide you at each step of the way.'

This was all very reassuring. 'OK,' I said. 'So all I need to find out now is what Step One is.'

Suddenly there was a strange feeling of a presence in the car.

'Do you feel something like a spirit — like a third person in here with us?' asked Raymond quietly.

'Yes, I do,' I said, even more quietly. 'Do you think it could be ... could it be God?'

'Maybe it is.'

Our whispers gave way to silence. We both experienced mixed feelings of awe and excitement, tinged with fear.

Then I said hesitantly, 'I'm getting these really strange waves of shivers running from the top of my head right down to the bottom of my spine.'

'So am I,' said Raymond. 'It's kind of scary, isn't it?'

'Yeah. I don't fancy driving home on my own!'

But the time came for me to leave, and so we parted, wondering about it all. It was an eerie drive home, and I confess to looking over my shoulder a number of times to make sure there was no ghost on the back seat — not that I believe in ghosts! When I arrived home, I prayerfully opened my Bible, and Jeremiah 50:2 caught my attention: 'Announce and proclaim among the nations, lift up a banner and proclaim it; keep nothing back.' Again I felt the strange presence and the shivers, but this time I wasn't scared. I knew that this was a word to me from God. Somehow he wanted me to announce and proclaim his gospel among the nations. As time went by, it became clear to me that at some point in the future I should go into training for missionary work. So God had shown me what Step One was.

After I left school, I worked for three and a half years in the Northern Ireland Housing Executive. Towards the end of this period as a public servant I was accepted to study for a primary degree at the Ulster Polytechnic, and around the same time I applied to become a student for the ministry of the Presbyterian Church in Ireland. My intention was to obtain my theological training through the church and then go into overseas missionary work. (Students for the Presbyterian ministry in Ireland take a primary degree first, in any subject, followed by a theological qualification.) At the Polytechnic I decided to read Sociology during the second and third years, even though it had been my worst first-year subject, because I wanted to learn about Marxism, the sociology of religion and the sociological (as opposed to theological) explanation of deviant behaviour. As a full-time student, I had long summer holidays, and this gave me an opportunity to get involved in various Christian activities and to travel extensively in Europe. On two occasions I was involved in Christian ministry to believers in the Communist countries of Eastern Europe.

During my time at Polytechnic my Christian faith continued to deepen and develop and, in particular, I began to feel a profound concern for the people of the Third World. As a Christian, I was appalled by the fact that for so many millions of people living on this planet, life consisted of a mere struggle for survival. It was a fight against poverty and disease — in short, it was unremitting misery. Reading through the Bible, I was encouraged and challenged by the realisation that God is deeply interested in and concerned for the physical needs of people, as well as for their spiritual needs (although ultimately man's spiritual needs have the priority). My sociology course contained a good deal of Marxist ideology and materialistic philosophy, in which any spiritual reality was implied to be a mere figment of the imagination and 'the opium of the people', so it was helpful for me to have a solid biblical foundation for my thinking, which showed me that Marx and the Communists were not the first ones to be concerned about the physical needs of the poor.

In fact I was so interested in God's social welfare programme that I did my degree thesis on the social organisation of ancient Israel. In preparing this it became very clear to me just how concerned God is that the poor, who do not have land to grow food for themselves, should have their needs met. It was a real shot in the arm for a Christian studying Marxism to know that God made provision for the fatherless, the widows and the aliens in Israel by creating the law of tithing. Also, it was thrilling to read that the prophets of the Old Testament were speaking out in the strongest possible terms against the exploitation of the poor by the rich.

Jesus demonstrated that God is concerned for the whole of the human person by not only achieving spiritual salvation for us through the cross and the Resurrection, but also by healing the sick and feeding the hungry. He carried the social priorities of the Old Testament into the New Testament when he said that the greatest commandment after loving God with all one's being was to love one's neighbour as oneself. This challenged me. I had to love my neighbour, but in this modern world, with instantaneous communication between all corners of the globe, who is my neighbour? I came to the conclusion that anyone and everyone on the face of the planet is in reality my neighbour, and so I must love him and try to help him, whether he be a peasant farmer living on the breadline in South America or a refugee in some war-torn part of Africa or Asia.

So I became involved with an organisation called Tear

Fund (The Evangelical Alliance Relief Fund), which I saw as a legitimate avenue through which to channel my concern for the poor of the world in a practical and financial way. Tear Fund is a Christian agency which brings relief and development aid to those in need, and since Jesus reminds us that 'man does not live on bread alone' (Mt 4:4), it also seeks to bring spiritual food to the recipients of its aid.

Over the years I had sometimes toyed with the madcap idea of cycling around the world, so that I could see for myself some of the fascinating places which I had previously only heard or read about. I had been a keen cyclist since my school-days, so to me a bicycle naturally seemed the best way to get around the globe. It would be a good way to meet ordinary people, it was cheap (almost free) and it would be a taste of real adventure. Just imagine cycling through a desert, all loaded up with bags, supplies and water; or through a jungle full of strange animals and weird noises. What an experience it would be to cross the Rocky Mountains by bike, and even to ride from one coast of the USA to the other. What a thrill to cycle into some of the most colourful cities of the world: Athens, Delhi, Kathmandu, Bangkok, Toronto. And what a variety of people I should meet: the rich American businessman, the Chinese drinks vendor, the aged Pakistani villager, all with their stories to tell of the great theatre of life.

But whenever I thought about all this, I told myself that it was just an outlandish fantasy and that it would never happen. And yet the idea would never go away altogether. Moreover, towards the end of my time at the Polytechnic, I began to wonder if somehow I might be able to use a cycling tour around the world to draw the attention of the general public and of Christians in particular to the needs of the people of the Third World. No matter how hard I tried to tell myself that it was all a crazy dream, the idea continued to develop at the back of my mind.

Also, it was clear to me that the time immediately after the end of my Polytechnic course would be my last chance to undertake such a trip. I had to go before starting my theological studies. After that I should be expected to settle down, conform and be sensible! If I was going to do this thing at all, I should have to do it soon, so I needed to make a decision about it.

Sometimes I shared these thoughts with my friends, but they usually dismissed the round-the-world cycle trip as just another of my mad notions! However, all that changed one morning in March 1981 as they and I sat in the Polytechnic's coffee bar, killing time before the next lecture by discussing my idea. There was Eddie, a student for the ministry like myself, married with three children. Then there was Steve, engaged to be married and intending to go into the legal profession. Finally, there was Alfie, a kind of Woody Allen character, full of wit and fun and jokingly accused by his friends of being a radical. He too was married and settled.

'Are you really serious about this cycle trip of yours?' asked Steve.

'Well, yes — I think so,' I replied. 'But I've got one big problem: where is the money going to come from?'

'Well,' said Eddie, always with an eye to business, 'if the whole thing were properly organised, you could probably get sponsorship from local firms.'

'That sounds like a big undertaking,' I said, 'but maybe it would be the right way to go about it.'

'You know, the more I think about this, the more it sounds like a good idea to me,' said Steve. 'Ever since I've known you, John, you've had a concern for the Third World. This trip could be a great opportunity for you to see the developing countries at first hand and find out what they're really like.'

'And when you get back,' said Eddie, 'you could go around showing slides, talking about the trip and encouraging people to support overseas development work.'

'Well, at the very least it sounds like a great way to get rid of you for a year!' said Alfie with his usual dry humour. 'Do you think you could make it two?'

'Thanks, Alfie,' I replied, grinning. 'It's nice to know I'm wanted!'

Then it was time for our lectures to start, and so we parted company.

A few days after our last conversation, my friends and I were again chatting and drinking coffee between lectures. Eddie had a suggestion to make: 'Why don't you make your round-the-world cycle trip a big money-raising venture for Tear Fund?'

'That's a great idea!' I said. 'It's so obvious — why didn't I think of it?'

'Let's work out roughly how long it would take to go around the world on a bike,' said Steve.

I started doing a few lightning calculations. 'I reckon I could cover about 50 miles a day — that's 300 miles a week, 1,200 miles a month. That would allow me plenty of time to be out of the saddle, take photographs and meet people. I'm sure I could get around the world in a year.'

By now, Alfie was beginning to get in on the act. 'But what about the lolly?' he asked.

'Well,' I replied, 'on my previous cycling trips £5 a day has been enough for my food, accommodation and day-to-day purchases. So we need to allow £1,800 for that. Add to that another £1,200 for air fares, insurance and equipment, and it looks as though £3,000 in total will be enough.' I laughed. 'But where am I going to get £3,000?'

'There's something else you should consider, too,' said

Eddie. 'Don't you think you ought to have a travelling companion, if only to reduce the anxiety for your family?'

'You're right,' I agreed, 'I do need someone to come with me. But who? I can't think of anyone right now.'

Our conference came to an abrupt end as we once again went off to our lectures.

I continued with my studies, but the idea of the round-the-world trip remained an occasional talking-point at coffee breaks. One evening I took out my old school atlas and started planning. This atlas was especially useful because it gave rainfall and temperature statistics for most areas of the world. I worked out that I would need to cycle around the world in an easterly direction in order to take advantage of the prevailing winds. I would need to leave in late August or early September and head south to the hot countries for the winter, then go up to the northern states of the USA in the summer. It also became clear to me that I would need to be out of South-East Asia by mid-June, when the monsoon rains would make cycling impossible.

It took me about half an hour to work out a likely route. Starting in Ireland, I would go through England, Belgium, Holland, West Germany, Austria, Yugoslavia and Greece. Travelling from there to Pakistan presented a problem because the traditional route to the East, through Iran and Afghanistan, was now out of bounds. I knew there was a passenger-boat service between the Persian Gulf and Karachi and that I would be able to cycle from Greece to Iraq through Turkey and Syria, but it would then not be possible to reach the Gulf, because of the war between Iraq and Iran. However, there was another way: to go by boat from Greece to Israel, cycle to Egypt and then hitch a lift at Suez on a ship headed for Karachi. If the worst came to the worst, I could always fly to Karachi from Athens or Cairo.

From Pakistan, the probable route would be through North India, Nepal and Bangladesh. But I wasn't too sure where I could go after that. If it was at all possible, I would like to go on into China, but it was very unlikely that this would be allowed, despite the liberalisation of China in recent years. And I was told by the Burmese Embassy that even though roads into Burma were marked on the map, they were overgrown and dangerous. The government would not be able to guarantee my safety in the border districts. So it looked as though I would have to take the east coast of India down to Sri Lanka, go by boat to Singapore and cycle through Malaysia and Thailand. Then I would fly to the west coast of the USA and cycle across the continent to New York. From there, I would fly on to Ireland. That worked out at about 15,000 miles in all, and I reckoned that if all went well, it could be done in a year.

But who would come with me, and how would we raise £6,000 to cover our expenses? These were major obstacles to overcome.

2

Departure

Despite periodic fluctuations of enthusiasm, the idea lived on. It would not die. One day I went into the Tear Fund office in the centre of Belfast to get the initial reaction of Graham Fairbairn, the then Regional Organiser, before going any further. I was not entirely unknown to him. He knew I was a keen cyclist and a Tear Fund supporter. He welcomed me and brought me into his office.

'How can I help you, John?' he enquired.

'Well ...' I replied hesitantly, 'I hope you don't have a weak heart or anything like that!'

'No, I don't think so,' said Graham, amused and puzzled. 'Why do you ask? Have you got something really shocking to tell me?'

'The truth is, I'm thinking about cycling around the world, partly to raise money for Tear Fund. I'd like to know what you think about the idea.'

Graham was stunned. 'Sorry?'

'I'm studying for the Presbyterian ministry and in June I'll be finishing my primary degree at the Poly. I'm thinking of taking a year off to cycle around the globe, to see the Third World and to raise some money for Tear Fund.'

Graham was still stunned. 'Really? ...'

'Yes. I just wondered how Tear Fund would feel about it.'

At a later date Graham confessed to thinking at the time, 'Oh no — we've got a right mad hatter here!' But right now he kept that thought to himself. 'Well, John ... er ... at this stage I wouldn't want to encourage or discourage you,' he said. 'I'm not quite sure what to think about the idea, to be honest. In a way it's entirely up to you what you do, and if you give any money you raise to Tear Fund, we'll be very pleased to receive it.'

'Of course, things are only at a very early stage at the moment, and I'm just testing the waters,' I said. Graham listened intently as I explained my idea in greater depth. Finally I said, 'At the moment I have two major obstacles to overcome: I need someone to come with me, and we'll need £6,000 to cover our costs.'

'H'mm. Well, if you're serious, John, I'll try to help. I've got some contacts in the business and student communities, so I'll make your needs known. You'll keep me in touch, won't you?'

That was the most Graham could do for me at that stage, but as the project developed he was able to give it his full blessing.

From then on, I started to pray more earnestly about the whole idea. As a Christian, I believed that if I sincerely wanted to know God's will for me, praying was one way of finding out. I prayed specifically that he would show me quite clearly whether this trip round the world was the right thing for me to do that year or not. I also asked God to provide a partner for me by the end of April. My family and friends needed to be reassured about my safety, because on a journey around the globe all sorts of unpleasant things could happen, such as violent attack or sickness. So my friends at the Polytechnic started to spread the word.

One Sunday afternoon in April, I bumped into John Rodgers, who, like me, was a member of Dungannon

Presbyterian Church. He was the son of the minister and worked for a car components retail firm.

'Remember that idea about cycling around the world you mentioned to me last Sunday?' he asked. 'Well, I'd like to hear some more about it.'

So a few days later we met and discussed it, and I told John my plans. But to be quite honest, I was not all that happy about his interest in coming with me. For a start, he was six and a half years younger than I. Also, he didn't have a passion for cycling. I thought we didn't have enough in common. However, we did have the most important thing of all in common: we were both Christians.

I did not actively encourage him to come with me, as I knew full well that the proposed trip would be fraught with dangers and that there would be a fair chance of one or both of us getting injured or even killed during the year away. So the onus was on him to take the initiative. The decision was not mine, but was between John, his family and God. If John was the person God had chosen to accompany me, then I was happy. Anyway, one of my prayers had been answered: God had provided a potential partner for me before the end of April. But we still needed all that money!

Now that it looked as if we really might attempt to cycle around the world, our parents naturally began to show some signs of anxiety. So they, John and I got together one evening to talk the matter over. We really appreciated our parents' concern about our well-being, and we wanted to do our best to allay their fears. Most of the questions were aimed at me, since I was the originator of the whole idea. As our minister, John's father took a leading role in expressing the parents' concern and in articulating many questions.

'Let's get this straight at the start,' he said. 'How serious are you two about this project?'

'Yes, we really are serious,' I replied, 'though if there are any problems we haven't thought about yet, we want to face them.'

Mr Rodgers asked his son, 'John, have you thought about the fact that your employers will find a replacement for you while you're away, and that when you come back you'll have no job?'

'Yes, I've thought about that,' replied John. 'But I think it's worth giving up my job for this project.'

'Before we go any further,' said Mrs Rodgers, 'what is the aim of the project?'

'We have three main aims in cycling around the world,' I replied. 'First, we want to draw the public's attention to world poverty; secondly, we want to raise money for Tear Fund's work among refugees in Thailand; thirdly, when we return from our journey we want to encourage Christians to see and fulfil their responsibility to those in need around the world.'

My mother asked us, 'Have you considered the danger you'll be exposing yourselves to? Cyclists are always vulnerable, and you'll be cycling on some very bad roads. Then there's the danger from thieves and bandits, not to mention the threat of disease!'

'We'll take all the precautions we possibly can,' I assured her. 'We'll take vaccinations and we'll cycle carefully. Most importantly, we'll pray that God will take care of us. Anyway, living in Northern Ireland can be dangerous too — for that matter, there's danger involved in living anywhere.'

'But what about wars — what about bad weather?' persisted my mother.

'We don't intend to go into any dangerous situations, so places like Afghanistan are out of the question. And as for weather, I've planned our journey carefully so that we'll avoid anything really bad. Believe me, I've thoroughly planned the whole project, including the route, the departure time, the cost, visas, innoculations — the whole works.'

'Look, boys,' put in Mrs Rodgers, 'we can all see that the idea and the motives behind it are good, and we all have confidence in your ability to see the journey through. But if this scheme goes ahead, you're going to need an awful lot of help in organising it — especially at this end while you're away.'

'Yes, I've thought of that,' I replied. 'We'll need a committee to carry the load for us. We could do with a few volunteers right away — all of you would do for a start!'

I had meant this as a joke, but our parents weren't very amused. However, their questions were being answered one by one and their initial fears were being gradually eased. But they still had one really important question to ask.

'But have you thought about how you're going to raise the money to pay for this expedition?' asked Mr Rodgers.

'Well, I reckon we'll need about £6,000,' I answered a little sheepishly. 'I'm sure we can raise it somehow.'

Our parents were not convinced.

John had let me carry the can so far, and now he jumped into the fray at the crucial moment. He was embarking on a career in business, and now made use of his knowledge: 'John and I can raise £1,000 between us,' he said, 'and I know that many businesses set aside funds for charitable purposes. I reckon we could raise a lot of money from firms in the Dungannon area alone, and on top of that we could approach others in Belfast and elsewhere in Northern Ireland.'

'I'm sure that when business people hear about the project, many of them will be generous to two local lads who are trying to help people in the Third World,' I added. 'I believe we can raise the £6,000!'

'All right, but the onus is on you to prove it!' said Mr Rodgers.

'OK,' I said. 'We will!'

And so ended the meeting. Our parents were slightly reassured by our answers to their questions, and we really felt that the pressure was now on to raise the money.

The whole project was shelved for a month while I took my final exams. Then we both rolled up our sleeves and got stuck in. There wasn't a minute to lose. We composed a letter to be sent to business people, together with a covering letter from Tear Fund confirming that we were genuine. It was now the end of May, so we prayed that if it was God's will for us to go ahead with the trip, £5,000 of the £6,000 we needed would be firmly promised by the end of June. If that happened, the biggest hurdle would be overcome and the trip would be on. If the money was not forthcoming by then, all our plans would be to no avail.

June was a month of frantic activity. In between writing letters to embassies, cycle manufacturers, the Cyclists' Touring Club and government departments, I was out in Dungannon and its surrounding villages with John, visiting business people in an attempt to solicit financial support for the venture. As we expected, the reaction varied greatly, ranging from a cold shoulder to enthusiastic support. Most of the local businessmen were keen and asked us a lot about our project. One firm replied promptly with a £500 cheque; a certain wealthy businessman gave us a mere £2, just to get rid of us! We left the letters with those we visited and said we would call back at the end of June, when a final decision about the trip would be made on the basis of the promises of financial and material support we had by then received.

We felt we needed to make a promising start to our collection of funds in order to boost our confidence, so when the time came to visit the business people again we first of all called on those potential contributors who had been enthusiastic about the proposed venture and had been thinking in terms of at least £100. Most of them were just as generous as we had hoped they would be, with the result that our confidence was indeed boosted and a healthy precedent was set for subsequent contributors. We soon secured many £100 contributions and even a few of £200 or more. There were also many gifts of under £100. Each day the promises came in, sometimes in a rush, sometimes in dribs and drabs.

John and I had promised £500 each, and our families generously agreed to meet our contributions pound for pound. We knew it was going to be a close-run thing, but when at the end of June we added up the money which had by then been promised, the total came to just over £5,000! So another prayer had been answered, and suddenly the trip was on. We had got the green light from God. For the first time, I really believed that it was going to happen. But even at this stage many battles still lay ahead.

In mid-July another family meeting was held to decide what the next step should be.

'Well, I must say you two lads have done very well,' said my mother with genuine enthusiasm. 'I didn't really believe it would happen, but you've raised the money you need. I don't think there'll be any stopping you now!'

'Yes, congratulations are certainly in order,' said Mr Rodgers, 'but let's not get too carried away. There are still some questions to be considered. For instance, have you two fellows gone on any trips together yet, just to see how you get on?'

'Er — well — no, we haven't,' I answered.

'And you're thinking of spending a whole year in very close company and in extremely difficult and uncomfortable conditions? I think you ought to spend at least a few days together first.'

'Yes, that sounds like a very good idea,' I said. 'What do you think, John?'

'Sure,' he replied. 'I think it would be good to have a practice run. How about this coming weekend?'

So it was that a few days later we loaded up our bikes and cycled the forty miles to the youth hostel at Learmount Castle in the Sperrin Mountains. It was a cold, wet weekend and we got soaked to the skin both going and returning. There were no hot showers or even electric lights in the hostel. This meant that the conditions were as tough and uncomfortable as we could find on a July weekend in Ireland. We got on well together throughout this trip, and on returning home came to the conclusion that after such a test we could feel reasonably confident about being able to get on with each other during a much longer journey.

The hurdles in the way of the trip had been overcome, the money had been promised and it was green lights all the way. But we now needed to move quickly, because we had to set off by mid-September at the latest, or we could run into bad weather in Europe. Then we needed to be in the hot countries of Asia during winter. It was clear that if we were to get away in time, and if the project were to be handled properly while we were away, we would need a committee.

By this stage, I was beginning to feel the pressure. There was so much preparation to be done and, as the whole project was my brainchild, I was conscious that if it should fail, the blame would rest firmly upon my shoulders. So it was a great relief to be able to hand over much of the responsibility to the Committee of the Third World Cycle Expedition. This was made up of businessmen, teachers, housewives, a clergyman and a doctor. The Committee worked very competently on our behalf, but seeing my precious ideas taken out of my hands and tossed around by other people sometimes made me feel a little uneasy! Nevertheless, the Committee was a great source of encouragement and support to John and me, and their wisdom helped to offset the ill effects of the rash decisions which our youthful enthusiasm sometimes led us to make.

As we wanted our trip to be a purely Northern Ireland project, we decided to approach the Londonderry-based makers of Viking Bicycles to see if they would be willing to supply us with two Viking Clubman bikes for the journey. This model was built to a high specification, using only the best components. The manufacturers were keen to help, and let us have the bikes for half the usual price.

I asked for some modifications to be made. I wanted top-quality saddles. This was very important, because they would be the only source of comfort at times — cheaper saddles would have been a source of discomfort instead! Also, I wanted the wheel rims to be changed from alloy to steel, so that in the event of a disaster the steel rim could be kicked into some sort of circular shape, allowing us to continue our journey until a better job could be done. Finally, I was unhappy with the quick-release mechanism which allowed the wheels to be swiftly detached from the frame. It was obviously less secure than ordinary, no-nonsense bolt-on wheels — a fact we might come to regret in parts of the world where honesty was at a premium. A bike is not much use with only one wheel!

There were many small but essential preparations to be made and numerous pieces of equipment to be acquired, such as a tent, sleeping-bags, a stove and dishes. Then there were medical precautions to be taken, including a series of vaccinations. A medical kit, together with instructions, was put together for us. Finally, we applied for our American visas at the Belfast Consulate and were required to state that we would not work or raise money in the States while we were there. We were now ready to go, and the starting date was set: Tuesday 15th September.

The whole project was now public knowledge, and early in September our local paper carried an initial story on the planned trip. We were also asked to speak at a conference organised by the Crusaders youth movement and at a Festival for Presbyterian Youth. At these events we encouraged youth groups to take up our project in the coming year. As 15th September drew nearer, we were interviewed on BBC local radio, and on the Sunday before our departure a valedictory service was held in our church.

The day before we set off was hectic, as one would expect. We spent much of the day loading up our bikes, frequently and pleasantly interrupted by friends calling in to wish us well. We had been accumulating items we would need for months, and now they were spread out all over our bedrooms. Somehow we had to pack away all of them! Both John and I had four panniers on our bikes — two on each wheel. In addition to this we carried on our handlebars large saddlebags containing all our valuables and essential documents. These bags could easily be removed and taken with us when we left our bikes chained up somewhere. My bike had a saddlebag suspended from the saddle, and instead of a saddlebag John carried the tent in which we would spend many of our nights on the trip.

As I went to my familiar old bed that night, I wondered if I would ever sleep in it again! But I couldn't help being excited about setting off tomorrow to see the world and to fulfil the dream of a lifetime.

At last the great day dawned, and I donned my white Tear Fund T-shirt and black cycle shorts. After a normal breakfast, I weighed in at 142 pounds. The bicycle and its equipment weighed in at 77 pounds, which was a little too much for comfort. Then it was time to get on the bike — something I would get very used to over the next year or so.

As I cycled into Dungannon, I felt a little self-conscious, aware of the negative attitude of some people towards our project and of the admiration of others. John and I met up and cycled to the Market Square for a public send-off. As we rode into the Square, we were clapped and cheered by about a thousand well-wishers. Dr William Craig, a former Moderator of the Presbyterian Church in Ireland, conducted a short ceremony, with music led by the Dungannon Silver Band. Then the Third World Cycle Expedition was officially launched, and we were off on a trip that, all being well, would take us right round the globe in twelve months.

The first part of our journey was spent cycling in typically Irish weather as we made our way to Belfast through wind and rain. The next day, after many press photographs and interviews, we cycled down to the terminal of the ferry which would take us across the Irish Sea to Liverpool. There we said goodbye to our relatives and friends who had come to see us off Ireland's shores. It was an intensely emotional occasion, and we were all painfully aware that we might not meet again. The parting was particularly difficult for our mothers, who were clearly going to experience an anxious year. John and I would know at any given time whether we were safe or not, but our mothers wouldn't. I was deeply aware of the heartache I was causing, and this was my greatest regret.

After a final round of good wishes, handshakes, hugs

and tears we wheeled our two heavily laden bicycles through the terminal's security gate, waved a final goodbye and were gone. Sitting on the Ulster Princess as she sailed down Belfast Lough, I could not help but wonder about the wisdom of the whole trip. I suddenly felt the awful burden of responsibility on my shoulders again and became keenly aware of the many dangers that must lie ahead. But there was no way out now. We couldn't turn back. But still I wondered, 'Am I doing the right thing?'

I went to our cabin and opened the Bible given to me to take around the world by my lifelong friend Raymond and his wife, Sharon. I looked up the verses they had marked for me to read. They were Judges 18: 5–6, and recorded a conversation between five travellers from the Israelite tribe of Dan and a young Levite priest. The travellers asked, 'Please enquire of God to learn whether our journey will be successful.' The priest's verdict was, 'Go in peace. Your journey has the Lord's approval.'

That night I slept soundly. In the morning I resolved not to look back. Ireland lay a year and thousands of miles ahead. I was now eager to set out on the great adventure of cycling around the world.

3
From Liverpool to Athens

The Ulster Princess arrived in Liverpool the next morning, and then we set out across England, aiming for Dover, staying at youth hostels and camping out along the way. England threw the worst of its weather at us. Between Canterbury and Dover, we were assaulted by torrential rain and gale-force winds which whipped at us from the west. The rain seemed to be 'falling' horizontally, lashing straight into our faces. 'Roll on sunny Greece!' I thought.

This little jaunt across England was a valuable piece of training for us, and we began to get accustomed to riding bikes weighing all of seventy-seven pounds. Keeping the bikes moving on the level wasn't difficult, as their considerable mass gave them a great deal of momentum, but we had problems whenever we came to a hill! Then the momentum disappeared and the speed died as we dropped to the lowest of the ten gears. To begin with we just had to admit defeat and walk up the hills. However, we adopted a positive attitude, reminding ourselves that all the time we were getting fitter and stronger, and would soon be able to sail over hills like these.

We also got the chance to make use of our camping equipment. Like all of our gear, it was of the highest quality. It had to be. After all, it would have to last a year in temperatures varying between below freezing-point and above 100 degrees Fahrenheit, in conditions ranging from cold, wet environments to hot, humid tropics. We unpacked the micro-weight tent and erected it for the first time. There was just room enough in it for both of us. The fly-sheet had two large bell ends under which we could put all our bags and even the bikes. The real valuables — such as passports, money, cameras and the short-wave radio — were kept in the bags attached to the handlebars, and they would always come with us into the sleeping compartment at night.

Our journey to Dover also gave us the opportunity to try out our culinary skills, which would have to sustain us all over the world during the next year. Frequently on our rough-and-ready menu were delights such as beefburgers, fried eggs and baked beans. We knew that as long as we had some baked beans, we would not starve! We were never quite reduced to the monotony of eating beans for breakfast, lunch and dinner in the same day, but we got quite close to it at times. Long live the baked bean, that most dependable of foods! For our lunches, we usually had sandwiches and milk, with high-glucose confectionery and fruit every two hours between meals. This helped us to keep our energy levels up and to make good progress.

On Thursday, a week after we had set off, we caught the ferry from Dover, and so we left the English-speaking world. If all went well, we would be away from it for all of nine months until we reached the USA or Canada.

On arriving at Ostend, we passed through the passport control — the first of many we would see in the months to come. Next morning we set off on our journey across the Continent, cycling for the first time on the right-hand side of the road. It's quite a pleasure cycling in Belgium, as the country has a good network of cycleways, most of which run alongside the roads. However, the condition of these varies from smooth tarmac to roughly joined concrete slabs or cobblestones — these can make travelling very bumpy if you're riding a bike and load weighing five and a half stone! Still, it's very pleasant to be away from the traffic and exhaust fumes, and it's a special pleasure to have priority over other road users at junctions.

We usually spent our nights at youth hostels on our journey across Europe. They are interesting places and tend to gather together under one roof fascinating if somewhat motley collections of travellers. We got to meet all kinds of people, of all ages and from all over the world. In Gent we were joined at our table at dinner-time by an untidily dressed elderly man wearing a black beret. Sipping his beer, he politely enquired into our travels. Where were we from? Where were we going? 'I come from Argentina,' he informed us, 'and have been travelling around Europe and the Middle East for the past year.' He sipped his beer again. 'In the new year I plan to travel to India, the largest democracy in the world.'

I wondered how he had the time to travel so widely. 'What's your job in Argentina?' I asked.

'I'm a professor of philosophy at a small university there,' he replied.

I had to admit that he did sound educated, but frankly, I didn't believe he was a professor. That sounded like a tall story to me! I was in a slightly mischievous mood, so I decided to test him.

'What's your assessment of Weber's thesis on the relationship between the Protestant work ethic and the spirit of capitalism?' I asked him, making use of the sociology I had learned at the Polytechnic. Let's see if he could answer that one!

However, without a qualm, he gave such a reply to my

question as to confirm without a doubt that he was indeed a professor. And so the three of us then settled down to a fascinating debate on religion, Marxist materialist philosophy and current world politics. You really do meet the most interesting people in youth hostels!

By Sunday, we had reached the Belgian capital, Brussels, and stopped off to see its sights. On Monday morning we headed out across the rather flat, boring Belgian countryside, making for the Dutch border. It was at this stage that we encountered some teething problems with the bikes. The outer chain wheel on John's bicycle had managed to work itself loose, but a conveniently located cycle shop was able to supply the necessary nuts and bolts for the repair. Also at this stage, John developed a problem with one of his knees, so we had to take things slowly for a few days. In the meantime, I managed to acquire the first puncture of the trip — the first of many, no doubt, I thought at the time. I was expecting to get as many as half a dozen punctures a day in countries like India and Bangladesh — but we were prepared for that, with six spare tubes and four spare tyres. But the Indian subcontinent was a long way off, and we had yet to cross many countries before reaching it. Mind you, we were passing through the countries quite quickly now. In fact we crossed Holland in an afternoon! On 29th September we had breakfast in Belgium, lunch in Holland and dinner in Germany, travelling all the way by bike. Not bad going! (Actually, it wasn't that great a feat of cycling, as our route via Genk [Belgium], Maastricht [Holland] and Aachen [Germany] took us through a part of Holland that was only fifteen miles wide!)

We were finding by this time that the traditional continental breakfast of coffee, a bread roll and jam or cheese wasn't enough to get us through a whole morning of cycling. Our Irish stomachs just didn't know how to cope with such meagre rations! So we usually supplemented it a little later along the road. In the evenings we were able to get quite good, reasonably priced meals at fast-food restaurants like McDonalds. A beefburger with chips, hot apple pie and strawberry milk-shake went down a treat! We also tried cooking our own meals at the youth hostels, doing our shopping at supermarkets. This was usually straightforward, but sometimes we made mistakes by not examining the labels written in foreign languages closely enough. One day I bought some coffee, thinking it was of the instant kind, only to discover later that it was the type for which one needs a percolator and filter! Needless to say, we had brought neither of those with us.

At Cologne in Germany we stopped off to see the magnificent Gothic cathedral and to visit the Tutankhamun exhibition. Then we headed south along the banks of the mighty Rhine river. The scenery here was much more attractive than in Belgium. There was the river and its many boats and barges to look at, either sweeping down towards the sea or chugging patiently against the unrelenting current. The banks were lined with quaint little villages and impressive cliffs. It was October now, and we were making for the warmth of the Mediterranean.

We continued to meet interesting people, though some of them were not as pleasant as we might have wished. One Sunday afternoon we met and chatted with an American couple. They then parked their bicycles and went away, with their bags containing their valuables still attached to the handlebars. Not surprisingly, when they returned, they discovered that they had been robbed, and promptly accused us of being the thieves!

'Come on, what have you done with our stuff?'

demanded the man. 'D'you think we were born yesterday? We know you took it!'

'Look, honestly,' I replied, trying not to get angry with him, 'we haven't been near your bikes. We haven't so much as touched them!'

'What's the matter? Do I look stupid or something?' said the man, getting increasingly irate. 'Where have you put our stuff? You'd better give it back, or we'll get the local police on to you!'

'I promise you,' I said firmly, 'we haven't taken your things. You can call the police if you like, but it won't make any difference. Look, if you don't believe me, you're quite welcome to search through all our bags. We've got nothing to hide.'

'Well, maybe I'll just do that,' said the man, going over to our bikes. He opened up our handlebar bags and rummaged around for a while. Puzzled, he pulled out two large books. 'What are these?' he asked.

'They're Bibles,' I replied, secretly rather amused, despite my annoyance.

The man's face fell in embarrassment. 'Bibles, huh?' he said. He replaced our valuables in their bags.

'Well — er — I guess you didn't steal our things,' he admitted gruffly, and walked away.

The German people we met were very kind and helpful, but it was Germany's roads that gave us problems. In Germany, it is the car which rules, and there is no preferential treatment for cyclists as there is in Belgium and Holland. Cycling on the autobahns is of course illegal, but in fact it was a real problem to find any road at all on which we were permitted to travel. This became a particular problem as we neared the heavily populated areas of Heidelberg and Stuttgart. But as we went south and got further away from the hazards of modern industrial society, things got easier and we began to look forward to the peace and quiet of the Alpine region. Peace and quiet, yes — but hard work too! Because ahead of us lay a great, unmovable barrier. The Alps blocked our path. There was no way round them; we would have to go through them.

At Ulm in southern Germany we crossed that other great European river, the Danube. Here it cuts north-east across Germany before turning sharply to the south-east at Regensburg and winding through Austria, Hungary and the Balkans, finally reaching the Black Sea. From then on, as we headed south to the Austrian border, the ground rose gently and the villages became increasingly Alpine in character. It was very quiet and peaceful here, with cows munching the lush green grass and the tinkling of their bells adding to the serene atmosphere of the region. Then we reached the brow of a hill, and quite suddenly the magnificent Alps came into view for the first time. They stretched right across the horizon fifty miles away, and the snow-capped peaks glistened majestically in the sun.

The mountains drew me on. My pace quickened and I felt a mounting excitement about the prospect of cycling through that land of inspiration. As we passed through the pre-Alpine forests and the picturesque villages of wooden houses attractively adorned with bright flowers in window-boxes, I could not help but wonder at the beauty of the world.

But just then, by stark contrast, two German jet fighters passed over us, their powerful engines screaming and leaving a trail of pollution across the otherwise idyllic scene. God's world was a beautiful place, but now my mind filled with thoughts of how man, in his sin and stupidity, had raped, plundered and despoiled that world.

Sitting by a stream eating my lunch, I watched the clean, pure water rushing by, on its way from the mountains to the valleys and plains below. My thoughts were troubled as I remembered the giant chemical plant we had seen downstream, which daily emptied thousands of gallons of poison into that same water, killing the fish and everything else, and all in the name of profit. I watched the cows contentedly chewing the cud, eating grass that with artificial fertilisers had been made to grow greener and faster than it naturally would have done. I noticed the big, muscular bulls, made unnaturally massive by the hormone injections and growth promoters which had been pumped into them in the name of profit. Then I thought of the problem of cancer, and wondered if it was caused by man's tampering with the natural order. I thought of the thousands of millions of people on our planet who are living in poverty, some of them dying of undernourishment; on our journey we would actually meet some of those people. And then I wondered how their fellow men could spend such vast amounts of money and resources on weapons, such as the jets which had just flown over us. Man is making such a mess of this beautiful world. 'Oh God,' I thought, 'what have we done?'

We switched on the radio, and the shocking news of the assassination of Egypt's President Sadat intensified my thinking about the stupidity and wickedness of mankind. The practical upshot of this tragic event for us was that it would probably be wise to avoid Egypt, since the country was now in a state of crisis.

Looking even further ahead, I wondered what I would be doing this time next year. I often wonder things like that. Maybe the trip would have to be called off at some stage, because of illness or accident. At the back of my mind was the chilling possibility that I might no longer be alive in a year's time. But if we arrived home as planned, then I would need a job that would allow me to spend my spare time going around the supporting groups back home, talking about our experiences on the cycle trip. Maybe I would be a petrol-pump attendant or a dustbin man! Time would tell.

We pressed on southwards. There were now mountains all around us and we were climbing steadily, into the colder air of the higher altitudes. We stopped for the night at the hostel at the border town of Mittenwald, and before going to bed I put on my waterproof anorak and went for a short walk, even though it was raining. I must have walked about a mile down the road that led to the valley below. Behind me the Alpine hostel looked warm and attractive, glowing with orange light, set amid the cold, wet, towering mountains. I was snug in my anorak.

Standing there, gazing at the scene, I prayed about all kinds of things: for our safety on the trip, for our folks at home, for guidance for the future. Then I felt someone's presence, and looked around. But no one was there. I was sure someone was there — but no. As I continued to talk inwardly to God, I became aware of a warm feeling coming over me, and then a sensation of my scalp tightening. Waves of shivers started running down my spine and I felt an intense inner joy. Feeling a little uneasy, yet very interested in the experience, I returned to the hostel wondering if this was a manifestation of God's presence.

The next morning we crossed the border into Austria and descended into the Innsbruck Valley. Within a few days, after straining our way up seemingly countless miles of winding mountain road, we passed over the top of the Alps, through a three-mile-long tunnel. Cyclists were not allowed through it, but we managed to hitch a lift for us and our bikes with a truck driver. Then we were on the southern side of the Alps, and it was now downhill all the way.

On entering Lienz near the Austrian-Yugoslav border, we had our first accident. We were cycling in the dark, moving rapidly downhill. Suddenly John, who was ahead of me, jammed his brakes on in order to read a sign telling us how to get to the youth hostel, but because his rear light wasn't working, I didn't notice that he had stopped and so ran my bike into the back of his. However, the next day I got my wheel fixed and John bought a new rear light. We decided to do no more cycling in the dark!

So the Alps were behind us, and we were rather pleased with ourselves at having crossed our first major geographical obstacle. But ahead lay Yugoslavia, a country with so many high mountains and steep roads that it was just as much of an obstacle as the Alps. It is said of Yugoslav road builders that they can build a road right up a wall. From my own experience, I knew that wasn't much of an exaggeration. I had been there quite a number of times during my travels around Europe. When involved in ministry to the Yugoslav churches, I had brought Bibles and other Christian literature with me into the country. Of course, this had all been quite legal and I had never had any trouble from the Yugoslav border police, but such activities did not have the approval of the government. The thought now occurred to me, with Yugoslavia staring me in the face, that maybe someone somewhere with red tendencies had passed on a report of my previous visits to the country to the police. Maybe somewhere in Yugoslavia there was now a file on a suspicious foreign character named John Hanson, and maybe instructions had been sent to all the border crossings that if he should try to enter Yugoslavia, he should be detained for a delightful little question-and-answer session. If the government knew that I had been meeting with Yugoslav Christians, they would be very interested to know who they were. I knew the chances of my being a marked man were very slim, but all the same, I found I couldn't help worrying about it. Languishing in a Yugoslav jail wouldn't exactly have been a nice way for our round-the-world trip to have ended!

From Lienz we set off for the Yugoslav border, taking a minor road that led us to the quite astonishingly steep Wurzen Pass. We rounded a corner, and there it was: a great big wall of tarmac rising at an unbelievable eighteen degrees! The Austrians, too, it seemed, were capable of building roads up walls! Beside the road were lanes of sand, in which runaway vehicles could stop safely. There were warning signs everywhere saying in five languages: 'GET INTO FIRST GEAR!' So we dropped into first gear, but, of course, it was no use. Even when we stood up on the pedals, our bikes still ran backwards! So we got off and pushed. It was a long, hard haul, and we had to stop every ten yards for a rest. But eventually we made it to the top and rounded a corner — and there, waiting for us, were the Yugoslav border police ...

We approached the border post slowly — it's not advisable to appear jerky at a sensitive border. I was feeling a bit nervous, so I chewed some gum. This was a minor entry point and there weren't many other travellers around, so our turn in the queue came quite quickly.

We walked the heavily laden bikes up to the border official, who wore a neat, grey uniform with a peaked cap. With suppressed alarm, I noticed the revolver at his hip.

'Passport!' he grunted ungraciously.

I had it ready and handed it over to him promptly.

'English?' he enquired.

I smiled in the affirmative, having no inclination to engage him in a debate about the intricacies of British citizenship.

He thumbed through my passport and, noticing that I

had been to his country before, asked, 'Yugoslavia good?'

I laughed with relief at this sign of friendliness and replied, 'Yes, Yugoslavia very good!'

He smiled, handed the closed passport to me and then went on to sort John out. I heard him pronounced 'English also' with approval.

Soon the formalities were over and we set off into the mountainous and beautiful province of Slovenia. Near the border the houses resembled those in Austria, but, as we drew further into the country, they took on a more characteristically Yugoslav look. They were often quite large, built out of attractive orange brick. Another thing we noticed early on was the roads, which left much to be desired. They were full of potholes and cycling on them was an arduous business.

Another unpleasant feature was the attitude of many of the people towards us. Until now, we had gone relatively unnoticed on our travels, but now we were like two fish out of water. It was obvious we were from the West, and often people would point, laugh and even shout at us. We felt uncomfortable, as if we were in a hostile environment. At the end of our first day in Yugoslavia, we stayed at the youth hostel in the beautiful lakeside resort of Bled. I had gone there a year before, after I had fled from Bucharest, having been roughed up by some drunken Romanian soldiers. Little did I know then that a year later I would be passing through Bled again on a bicycle and would be every bit as glad of the hostel. What a relief it was to get into that place and to see the friendly warden's face again. She remembered me, and said she was glad I had come back.

Once in Bled, we went out for a mixed grill and took the opportunity to assess our new environment. We were shocked by the contrast between it and the thoroughly Western atmosphere of Austria, and we even felt a twinge of homesickness. The place seemed unfriendly, few people spoke English and living conditions were austere.

Since the next day was Sunday, we decided to stay at Bled, resting and recovering from our culture shock. We spent the day boating on the lake, walking and visiting two local churches. As Christians, we felt it was right to take Sundays off, in order to give our bodies a rest one day in seven, to meet with some other Christians if possible and also to write to our families and friends at home. We felt we owed it to them to write home every Sunday without fail. At the end of each month we would write and post home an up-to-date account of our travels. We also planned to phone home, John one month, I the next.

A few days later we passed through Ljubljana, the capital of Slovenia, and then descended from its mountainous country down to the warm, arid coastline. Yugoslavia has the most beautiful coastline in Europe: white, limestone mountains sweep down to the sparkling, blue Adriatic Sea; brightly coloured shrubs and flowers grow among the hot boulders. And despite the dryness of the region, we found that it was full of wildlife. Blue and green dragonflies darted around us and, strangely, often flew at a fixed distance from our front wheels, giving us the odd sensation of being static. There were snakes on the roads and among the rocks, and many multicoloured birds wheeled and soared above us, their beautiful songs accompanied by the persistent murmur of the sea washing against the rocks on the shore.

The climate was one of extremes, however. Though it was usually dry, one afternoon we got caught in the most torrential cloudburst I have ever seen. The wind became so strong at one stage that cycling became impossible and we just had to hold our brakes tight, in case the wind should blow us off the road. However, once I had resigned myself to the prospect of becoming soaked to the skin, I decided to try to enjoy the power and beauty of the storm, and started up an impromptu rendition of 'Raindrops Keep Falling On My Head' at the top of my voice. John thought I'd finally gone bananas!

One of the things I relished about our time in Yugoslavia was the quality of their food. Every day John and I would buy a loaf of bread each from a bakery — straight out of the oven, all warm and soft, with no preservatives or artificial junk thrown in. This, I decided, was how all bread ought to taste. There was definitely something to be said for pure, simple, unadulterated food. The eggs we ate were good too, laid by healthy, happy free-range hens. These were real eggs, very different from the insipid, watery things which we get from those cruel, unnatural factory farms where thousands of hens are incarcerated in wire cages, without room to scratch and flap and lead a normal hen's life.

Usually we would boil up four eggs at a time in order to conserve fuel, and since we were now in an area where water needed to be sterilised, either by boiling or with purification tablets, I used the water that the eggs had been boiled in for brushing my teeth and rinsing my mouth out. It didn't taste any worse than water that had tablets dissolved in it, and it probably contained some valuable minerals and vitamins for good measure!

Finding accommodation at night was often a problem, since it was no longer the tourist season and most of the campsites and *sobes* (bed-and-breakfast houses) were closed. Each morning we had a short Bible reading from a book of meditations which a friend had given me and a short time of prayer when, among other things, we would ask for God's protection while we were on the roads and for somewhere to stay the night. One evening we arrived at the town of Pakostane and couldn't find anywhere at all to stay. So once we had done everything we could humanly do and had got nowhere, I realised that this was the sort of situation in which we should pray and ask for God's intervention. 'There's no point in having faith if you're not going to use it,' I thought. So silently I prayed, 'Lord, your handbook tells me that if I ask, it will be given to me; if I seek, I shall find; if I knock, it will be opened to me. We need somewhere to stay tonight. So I ask you to provide for that need.'

Twenty-five minutes later, John went to enquire at a *sobe*, as I had discovered that someone there spoke French. While John was inside, a young boy came up to me to take a look at my bike.

'Do you speak any English?' I asked. No reply except a friendly smile. Then I said, '*Sobe, sobe*?' a few times, pointing to the houses round about.

Soon John returned, looking disappointed and annoyed. 'They're trying to rip us off,' he said. 'They want us to pay 500 dinars to stay the night!' They were asking the equivalent of £8, which was an awful lot for bed and breakfast in Yugoslavia! We had absolutely no intention of paying that sort of money. So I tried the boy again: '*Sobe, sobe*?'

Now he got the message and started leading us somewhere. Eventually we reached a guest-house that was closed for the season, but the landlady very kindly said we could stay the night free! Much relieved, we gratefully gave the boy some chocolate and the lady some coffee we had bought in Germany.

Finding that house was really comforting after being without a place to lay our heads in a strange environment where no one could speak English. Later, sitting down to eat some chips, I wondered if my prayer had had any effect: had divine intervention occurred or had our finding accommodation been the result of chance or luck and been something which would have happened anyway? It had not been often in the past that I had found myself in an impossible situation and had been obliged to put my faith into action. But on a few occasions I had had to do it, and it had worked. It had worked once again tonight.

When we reached the southern limit of the Yugoslav coastline, we turned east and passed through the Republic of Montenegro (one of the several republics of which the state of Yugoslavia is composed) and by the end of October passed into the autonomous region of Kosovo in the Republic of Serbia. Reaching the town of Pec, we were suddenly aware of a change in the culture around us. There were many horses and carts on the rough, cobbled roads, driven by old men wearing little white skullcaps. Women led cows along the roadside in search of green pasture for them, while shepherds herded their flocks into the market-town. There were the mosques with their tall, narrow minarets, from which issued that eerie call to prayer. This was the first Muslim area we had so far encountered, and it came as a culture shock to us both. The sudden transition from a European environment to an Asian-type one was disorientating. To begin with the jostling crowds, the animals and the dozens of children chasing after us were quite frightening. However, really it was all quite similar to what we were to see in Pakistan, so the experience helped prepare us for the real East, which we would encounter in a few weeks' time.

Most of the animals we saw appeared to be well cared for, but sometimes we would see evidence of cruelty and neglect. I saw three very thin horses being taken out of an outhouse; they were in a state of severe malnourishment and the back of one of them was concave, its spine next to its pelvic girdle being almost vertical. I felt angry with the human monster who had done this to these intelligent, feeling creatures, and I felt I wanted to make that person suffer for his cruelty. On another occasion, I saw a bullock which had had one of its eyes gouged out. I consoled myself with my belief that God will judge us all for how we have treated or mistreated his creation.

But most of the people were kind to the animals and to us too. One evening, at the town of Gostivar, we arrived to find that the campsite and the hotel were full. Once again, I asked God to intervene and provide us with somewhere good and safe to spend the night. Cycling out of town, not knowing where we were going, we pulled up outside a house. Just then someone came out and in good English invited us in for food, showers and beds. He even invited us to come and watch European football on television! One moment we had been cold, hungry, tired, lost and anxious; the next we had warmth, friendliness, hospitality and even entertainment! I thanked God, and took note of the fact that when I asked him to help, he did.

By November, we had reached Greece and headed towards the great metropolis of Athens. Our route through this ancient land took us through the towns of Larisa, Lamia and Delphi, through highlands and many steep passes, through river valleys and carefully farmed and irrigated rolling countryside. We were glad of an uneventful ride to the capital, since we were anxious to get there as soon as possible in order to replenish our funds, get letters from home and investigate the different ways of getting to Pakistan.

At the youth hostel in Athens we met, among other colourful characters, an American who described cycling conditions in Egypt for us: 'Those drivers there, they're crazy! They drive real fast, ignore the lights and sometimes even drive on the sidewalks. Drivers there spend most of their time with one hand out of the window, shaking a fist at the other drivers, and the other hand on the horn. If you want my advice, I'd say Egypt's not the best place for you two guys to ride your bikes!'

This description certainly gave us food for thought and it, together with the prevailing unrest in Egypt and our wish to spend Christmas at a town in Pakistan called Rahim Yar Khan, where we knew some people, helped us to decide to avoid Israel and Egypt altogether and fly straight to Pakistan from Athens.

After visiting the historical monuments of Athens and savouring such Greek gourmet delights as *kebab* and *kataife*, we rode out to the airport, feeling apprehensive about leaving Europe — our continent. Greece was certainly foreign and was almost 2,000 miles from home, but at least it was European. To some extent it shared our own country's culture. But Pakistan and the rest of Asia would be a completely different ball-game, in a totally alien culture. When we made our final phone call home before catching our flight, it seemed as if we were saying goodbye for ever. The way we felt, we could just as easily have been going into outer space.

Finally we boarded the big, green Pakistan International Airlines DC10 and took our seats to the sound of whining engines, soft music and clicking seat-belts. The plane taxied to the runway and stopped, waiting for the signal to go. Sitting in my seat, I felt nervous about the flight and about the alien environment we would encounter at the other end of it. I suddenly had a sickening feeling of being trapped. I couldn't get out — couldn't escape from the culture shock which awaited me! But then, thinking that I was safe in the captain's hands, I realised I was also in the hands of one with even greater power to protect.

Suddenly the whine from the engines built up to a crescendo, the brakes were released and we sank deep into our seats as the great flying machine rushed down the runway. The nose lifted and we rose powerfully into the air. The white lights of Athens fell away beneath us as we climbed steeply and turned east, flying into the darkness of the night.

4
Pakistan

We were nearing the end of our flight. I peered through my window into the darkness outside. I could make out little specks of light down below: the towns and villages of Pakistan, scattered amid the sea of blackness like stars in the night sky. Mostly there was no pattern to these lights, but occasionally they formed clumps and sometimes lines. Over to the east, there was just the slightest hint of greyness where the black ground met the sky.

Then the tone of the engines changed and I could feel us lose speed and altitude. Inside the stewardesses in their long, green saris glided up and down the aisles, closing the lockers above our heads.

A feminine Pakistani voice came over the aircraft's public-address system: 'Ladies and gentlemen, we will be landing at Islamabad International Airport in about twenty minutes' time. Please extinguish your cigarettes and refrain from smoking until you are inside the terminal building. All passengers should now return to their seats, which should be in the upright position, and should fasten their seat-belts in preparation for landing. We hope you have enjoyed your flight with Pakistan International Airways.'

I obediently fastened my belt. Outside, I could now see two areas of bright lights looming towards us in the darkness. One was completely disorganised, like a plateful of illuminated spaghetti; I guessed that this was the old town of Rawalpindi. The other area of light was made up of lines running at right angles to one another; obviously this was the modern, planned city of Islamabad.

The plane lost height steadily, occasionally hitting some air turbulence. Soon we could see the lights of the road traffic below. The engine's pitch rose as the craft lay back into the wind and neared the ground. Below, the lights started rushing past as we bumped roughly on to the runway. The engines roared with reversed thrust, and the plane slowed and finally taxied to a halt. It was four o'clock in the morning and we had arrived in Pakistan, our first port of call in the great continent of Asia.

As I walked from the plane across the concrete of the runway, I thought with excitement, 'So this is Pakistan!' But it wasn't. We were still in the international environment of the airport, an artificial place of jet planes, travellers, high technology and terminal buildings. We wouldn't be in the real Pakistan until we got out of Karachi airport and set out across the country, and before that we had to take an internal flight from Islamabad in the north to Karachi in the south. Our plan was to eventually cross the border into India from the north, but we wanted to start our journey through Pakistan from the south in order to see as much of the country as possible. We planned to stop off on the way at Rahim Yar Khan, a town situated roughly halfway between Karachi and Lahore. We hoped to spend Christmas there with Lily Givans, a lady from our church back home in Dungannon who was working as a missionary for the International Christian Fellowship. The boys' hostel she was running had been built with the help of a Tear Fund grant, so that was an added reason for our wanting to see Lily and the work she was doing.

In the meantime, we had to pass through immigration and customs, so we waited at the luggage carousel like everyone else. The officials wore smart uniforms and had light brown skin and dark hair, and looked pretty much like airport officials anywhere in the world.

'First time in Pakistan, sir?' asked the one who dealt with me.

'Yes, that's right.'

After flicking through my passport and visas, he said, 'Welcome to Pakistan.'

After checking our bags in at the transit lounge, we sat around waiting for our flight to Karachi. At eight in the morning we were treated by the airline to tea, bread and cake. The tea was served in real china cups and was poured from a real china teapot. You wouldn't get service like that in Europe!

Outside it was bright and sunny now and I could see tall palm trees, with their long, branchless trunks and their clumps of narrow, stiff leaves at the top. We were now in a very hot, dry climate, and it would doubtless take some getting used to, I reflected.

Then it was time to board the plane for the hour-long flight to Karachi. During the journey I wandered about looking out of the windows, and was horrified by what I saw below: absolutely nothing! It all seemed to be one great big, grey desert. How on earth were we going to cycle through that? There was still desert all around as we landed at Karachi.

Stepping out of the plane into the bright sunshine was just like walking into a sauna — and this was just the beginning of December! How would we fare in similarly hot climates when April and May came around? I wondered what we had let ourselves in for.

Our bikes had come through the two flights in perfect

shape, and so we loaded all our bags on. Finally, after sending a telex to our folks at home, we were ready to go and stepped out of the terminal building into the real Pakistan.

The very first thing I noticed was the people — there were thousands of them bustling about. Some were wearing Western-style clothes, but most of the men were dressed in the traditional baggy trousers and the long, loose shirts that reach to the knee. The women were well covered up, wrapped loosely from head to foot in brightly coloured saris. This was a Muslim country, and women there did not show their ankles or arms and usually covered their heads. Almost immediately, we ran into the first of the beggars we were to see in Pakistan. He didn't have any legs, but managed to move about quite quickly by swinging his torso between his arms.

Everything was so bright and white. The walls of the buildings were white, many of the people's clothes were white and the bone-dry, dusty ground was white. The bright sunshine made the whiteness glare, so I had to get my sunglasses out.

Having taken in our surroundings a little, we decided to head out and face whatever Pakistan had to offer us. So we set off down the tree-lined avenue that led us away from the airport towards Karachi, the largest city in the country. At a junction on that busy dual carriageway a smartly dressed policeman, on noticing us, stopped the traffic and waved us on. We saluted him as we passed him, and he smiled and said, 'Welcome to Karachi.' It was encouraging to receive such courtesy and consideration.

One feature of Pakistani life which we disliked from the start was the traffic in the cities. That road to Karachi was very congested, noisy and polluted. There were a great many cars — some European, most Japanese — tearing about at high speed, braking, accelerating, blowing their horns and filling the air with choking fumes. There were also many small, overloaded buses which stopped and started every few hundred yards along the road and were to all appearances driven by racing drivers! There were lots of trucks too, all brightly coloured and churning out huge quantities of filthy blue and black fumes. And there were little three-wheeled scooter-like taxis, which made the harshest, roughest motor-bike noise imaginable and ripped in and out of the traffic, blowing their horns wildly. And, of course, there were literally thousands of cyclists, all riding bikes of the black, heavy old-fashioned type, adding the irate ringing of their bells to the hideous mêlée of noise. In among all this were we two bewildered Irishmen on our sophisticated touring cycles, receiving a fiery baptism into the culture of Pakistan.

However, the unpleasantness of Pakistan's traffic was compensated for by the friendliness of her people. Many waved to us and shouted, '*Salaam*!' Others pulled alongside us and, using what English they could command, would ask where we were from and where we were going. One man, dressed in traditional clothes, came alongside me on his bike and handed me an apple, smiling and gesturing as he did so. For a moment, I was suspicious, wondering if it was safe to accept the gift. No one had ever before shown such spontaneous courtesy to me, and so I didn't know what to make of it. But then I accepted the apple with a smile and a '*Salaam*', the only Urdu word I knew at that stage.

Finally we reached Karachi and checked in at the YMCA on Aiwan-e-Sadar Road. We were a bit shaken after that ride from the airport, and decided it would be a good idea to stay put for a week to adjust ourselves to the new cultural and climatic conditions. There would be a lot of new things to get used to now, not least the food. At the restaurant of the YMCA — an old building of yellow stone in the colonial style — we were able to eat Western dishes such as chicken, chips and boiled vegetables, but while we were staying there we also tried out some of the local specialities such as chicken *biryani*. Most Pakistani meals include a lot of rice and are highly spiced with hot peppers and chillies. Our stomachs never quite got used to the hot flavouring of Pakistani cuisine.

Something else we had to get used to was the wildlife of Pakistan. While we were eating at the YMCA, we met our first Asian rodents: a couple of fat rats ran along one side of the restaurant. And back in our room that evening we encountered a horrible, little grey lizard. It was about six inches long with a tapering tail and large eyes and was scampering about on the ceiling. This was an emergency! We couldn't possibly try to sleep with that creature in the room. So John ran downstairs and returned with the night watchman, who obligingly persuaded the lizard to go back out the way it had come and closed the window. We tipped him gratefully and breathed a sigh of relief. This sort of thing was going to take some getting used to!

We encountered many beggars on the streets of Karachi, but one man was particularly persistent in trying to get money from us. He had a snake in a basket, and as we approached, he started playing a pipe. The cobra rose up menacingly out of the basket, fixing its beady little eyes upon us. We didn't like snakes, so we turned away so as to avoid it. But the beggar wouldn't give up, and to our consternation he ran up the street and waited there for us. So we crossed over to the other side. But then the man simply followed suit and, throwing the basket down on the ground just in front of our feet, started playing his pipe again! We then realised that we were up against a determined man, so we gave in. We had no choice but to watch this piece of unwelcome entertainment. We kept well back from the snake and after a while gave the man a tip. He smiled ingratiatingly and thanked us. We hurried away, feeling greatly relieved.

We spent the first week of December in Karachi, and on Sunday 6th December we attended the evening English language service at Holy Trinity Cathedral. After the service, we chatted with the vicar, who was an Englishman. He gave us some very helpful tips on travelling in Pakistan: 'Remember that you will be vulnerable on bicycles. Pakistan is a violent country and some of the people are very poor. Because you're white, they'll think you're rich. Although most of the people are kind and will protect you, some are really desperately poor and could try to rob you. Just be careful and make friends with the local people wherever you can.'

He also gave us the address of the Anglican Bishop of Hyderabad, and suggested that when we got there, we should contact him, since he might be able to find us somewhere to spend the night. In fact, that contact turned out to be the beginning of a chain of contacts which ensured that we stayed with Christian people almost every night while we were in Pakistan.

Before leaving Karachi, we sent Christmas cards to our people at home, and then set off north for Rahim Yar Khan. We were to spend the next two weeks travelling through the province of Sind. I had seen the Sind Desert from the window of the plane which took us to Karachi, and now here we were on the ground, heading right into it. Sand stretched in all directions to the horizon, and the straight strip of tarmac we were travelling on divided the scene neatly in two.

However, the desert wasn't all sand; there were thorny bushes and shrubs dotted about here and there.

And there were people too, mostly living in tents or little brush houses beside the road, with a few goats nearby. After the cosmopolitan atmosphere of Karachi, this was a bit of a shock. I hadn't really expected to see conditions like this in Pakistan. It reminded me of what I thought Africa would look like, but not Asia.

It was hot in the desert — very, very hot. There were no trees under which to shelter and there was little vegetation to absorb the heat. Instead, the bright sand and the hot tarmac reflected the heat, making the atmosphere stifling. A cold drink would have been just what the doctor ordered, but it was so hot that the water we carried quickly became lukewarm. Sometimes we would call at the simple wayside tea-houses and would point hopefully at the rusted old Pepsi-Cola signs. But all they ever had to offer was empty bottles. What made it worse was that away in the south we could still see the delectably cool-looking waters of the Arabian sea, shimmering in the heat haze.

When we reached the desert town of Thatta, we hoped to be able to stay in the Rest House (composed of bungalows built by the British in colonial days) but discovered that we needed to book a room one month in advance. However, at the tourist office we got permission to camp at the back of the building. We didn't want to camp at all in Asia, since there were no proper campsites to be had and camping out in the wild would have been dangerous, but there just wasn't anywhere else for us to sleep in that town. And we were delighted to find that we would be camping next to a young German from Hamburg named Charles, who was also travelling by bicycle.

'Where are you making for?' I asked.

'I go to Hyderabad and then Bombay,' he replied. 'After that I cycle down the west coast and find myself a quiet beach. Then I will stay for some weeks and become brown. I will catch fish and sleep on the beach.'

'You seem very eager to get to India,' remarked John.

'Yes, I am,' admitted Charles. 'I want to get out of Pakistan, because although it is a very beautiful country, I think it is also a very dirty country.'

'Why do you think that is?' I asked.

'I do not know for sure. Maybe it is because it is a Muslim country.'

'Why do you say that?' asked John.

'Well, when I was in the Lebanon I could tell a Christian village from a Muslim one, because the Christian ones were usually cleaner.'

'Well, I've never been to the Lebanon,' I said, 'but I certainly do think that the people of Pakistan could do a lot more to help themselves with improved hygiene and sanitation.'

'That's right,' agreed John. 'In Karachi and here at Thatta we've seen great, big, stinking open sewers running along the sides of the streets.'

'Yes, it's no wonder there's so much disease about,' I added.

'I do not know why it is so,' said Charles, 'but the Christian countries seem to be cleaner and more prosperous.'

So the three of us spent the evening sitting cross-legged beside our tent, chatting and sipping Yugoslav herbal tea beneath a bright, moonlit sky.

The next morning the three of us set off again through the Sind Desert. The road was very hot and rough and was only a single track in places. We had also been warned that there were many poisonous snakes and dangerous black scorpions around, so we were careful whenever we stopped at the roadside.

On one occasion we all needed a drink, but discovered that we had run out of water. We noticed a little lake near the road. It was nearly dried up and looked very muddy.

'Do you reckon we could use some of that water?' I asked without enthusiasm.

'You must be joking!' said John. 'It's filthy! We can't drink that!'

'Do not worry,' said Charles. 'I have with me a filter pump, with which I will clean the water.'

So we went and got some of the dirty water. Charles put it through his filter, and then we boiled it for five minutes to kill the bacteria in it and finally mixed in a packet of vegetable soup, since we didn't really want to drink mere hot water. It was a strange experience, preparing soup in the middle of a sweltering desert! We poured it into three mugs and gingerly sat down to enjoy our roadside repast.

'Ugh!' exclaimed John after his first sip. 'The water is salt water!'

Charles and I cautiously sipped our own soup and came to the same unpalatable conclusion. We were now even more thirsty, so the search was on for Coca-Cola. I'm not particularly partial to the stuff myself, but it's one thing which you can find almost anywhere in the world — even in a desert in Pakistan. Finally we saw a Coca-Cola sign outside one of the little thatch-built shops which dotted the roadside. I went in, simply said, 'Coke,' and held three fingers up. The shopkeeper went to a large, round earthenware pot filled with cold water (there were no fridges out here!) and took out three bottles for us. We rapidly drank the contents of these, and then bought another three bottles.

Finally, two days after leaving Karachi, we crossed the great Indus River and reached the city of Hyderabad, a metropolis of a million people. We entered the city on a rather dilapidated dual carriageway, which had few road markings and in some places none at all. By degrees, we drew nearer the centre of the city, and found that the streets were narrow and packed with people and animals, like those of Karachi had been. The women always seemed to be busy, while the men were more likely to be sitting about! There were many well-attended mosques, and we frequently saw men stopping in the street at the call to prayer. Christianity in the city was rather unfavourably represented by a few very Western-looking churches which had been built in prominent positions during the colonial period.

We reckoned that if there was a tourist office in a mud-and-brick desert town like Thatta, there certainly ought to be one in a major city like Hyderabad. A few inquisitive people gathered around us when we stopped in the city, so we enquired, 'Tourist office? Tourist office?' Soon one young man was persuaded by his friends to help the hapless foreigners and set off on his bike with us following. We had been riding for some time when I began to suspect that we were going round in circles. 'There's something very familiar about these streets, and I'm sure we passed that mosque earlier,' I said to myself. Eventually we came to a halt in the centre of the city and in the negotiations which followed it became apparent that, in fact, there was no tourist office in Hyderabad and that we had just been taken on a conducted tour of the city.

While we were sorting all this out and trying to find someone who could speak English, the throng which was gathering around us, all interested in us and our bikes, grew to be several-hundred strong and soon completely blocked the road! Soon the adjoining streets had become a chaotic traffic jam: the place was packed with stationary carts, lorries and three-wheeler taxis, and the drivers of all of them were becoming increasingly irate with every passing moment. And all this was caused by two Irishmen and a German on their bikes!

'If we hang about here much longer we'll end up in jail for causing a public nuisance,' said John anxiously.

'I think you're right,' I agreed. 'We'd better act fast. But what should we do? Where can we go?'

'Are you wishing to go to American Centre?' asked one of the bystanders, trying to help us.

'The American Centre? Yes — let's go there,' I said. 'Will you take us there, please?'

'Yes, I take you,' replied the man, hopping on his bike and leading the way. And so, with relief, we slipped away out of the chaos.

Soon we arrived at the American Centre, which was a sort of social and cultural haven for Americans. It had its own English library and was in many ways a little bit of America right in the middle of Hyderabad. We planned to follow up the contact which the vicar in Karachi had given us, and to see if Bishop Jiwan of Hyderabad could help us to find somewhere to stay. A Pakistani boy at the American Centre said he knew where the Church of Pakistan compound was, and swiftly led us there. There we met Stewart Enthwistle, a missionary from New Zealand, who with Bishop Jiwan's permission allowed us to use the visitors' flat in the compound.

It was a real relief to be able to stay the night in this peaceful walled refuge. It was a little Christian island in the middle of a Muslim city. Even inside the compound the noises of that city intruded, especially at prayer times. There were half a dozen mosques nearby, and five times a day the call to prayer would go out on the loudspeakers. Then we would hear the now familiar words being bawled, barked, shrieked or beautifully intoned by hundreds of different voices: 'God is great. God is greatest. There is but one God, and Muhammad is the prophet of God.' All this took some getting used to, especially since it started at five in the morning!

While in Hyderabad, we took the opportunity to explore the place on foot. Like most Pakistani cities, it had a bazaar. This was a very colourful place. It was a maze of extremely narrow streets, full of tradesmen shouting out their prices, while people slapped hands together in settlement. Everything under the sun was sold there, including furniture, steel dishes, brightly coloured plastic buckets, exotic saris for the ladies, trinkets, key-rings, playing cards, fruit, vegetables, spices. I was interested to see some Erinmore tobacco, made in Belfast, on sale at one of the stalls. The bazaar was a place of loud noises and one of strong smells too. There was a lot of tobacco smoke, and traffic fumes and the odours of the spices on sale also permeated the atmosphere. And the open sewers running along the streets added their distinctive contribution to the general aroma!

I love animals, and I'm sorry to have to say that I was not impressed at all by the way they were treated in Pakistan. Many of the dogs were thin, had sores on their pelts and looked generally uncared for. The horses which pulled the passenger-carrying tongas were usually in good condition, although some looked underfed. One old horse, its ribcage showing through its loose coat, crawled along at a mere walking pace, such was its weakness. But it was the donkeys which seemed to receive the worst abuse. Great numbers of them were used to pull carts. Many of them were injured and limping, and I frequently saw them being kicked and beaten by their masters, who were heartlessly trying to make the poor animals pull their enormous loads a little faster. I saw one donkey with a broken leg, grazing pitifully on a patch of parched grass. There was to be no humane slaughter for this poor creature. No longer of use to anyone, it had simply been left to fend for itself. I saw another little donkey pulling a two-wheeled cart which bore such a long steel girder that it sagged and almost touched the ground at each end. The animal staggered along while its master, completely oblivious to its suffering, sat on the cart too. Finally the donkey collapsed with exhaustion. I felt deeply angry with the man who was inflicting such torture upon a dumb, innocent creature. Afraid that I would explode with rage and strike him, I had to turn and walk quickly away.

I was not sure who to blame for this appalling abuse of the animal kingdom. Initially I blamed Islam, believing that its ritual slaughter encouraged the people to generally mistreat their animals. For a while, I reacted by hating the Muslims and felt that their poverty was either a problem of their own making or was the just judgement of God. With contempt, I watched the chaos all around me: the disorganisation, the filth, the poverty, the noise. I wiped my shoes and with a feeling of relief stepped back into the clean, quiet environment of the Christian compound.

There I had the chance to think about what I had seen more rationally, and reflected that the people of the West are unkind to animals too. Many of our farming techniques are unnatural and distressful to them. We practise such cruelties as transporting livestock in cramped containers, incarcerating laying hens in tiny wire cages and imprisoning young calves in a dark environment in order to produce the delicacy of veal. And frequently people abandon pets when they are no longer required or when their novelty has worn off. So the Muslims are not the only ones who abuse their animals. Moreover, in a sense, the poor people of the world have more of an excuse than the people of the West, because they have to work their animals so hard just to feed their families; that little donkey pulling the enormous steel girder would have been indispensable to his master's livelihood. But the rich people of the world in many cases abuse animals for the sake of extra profit or mere convenience. However, even though I could think of excuses for the mistreatment of animals which I had just witnessed, I still found it hard to understand how a God of love could allow man to abuse innocent creatures in this way.

While we were at Hyderabad I celebrated my twenty-seventh birthday. I woke that morning to discover that John had very kindly bought me a copy of *Trinity*, a book by Leon Uris about Ireland. I really appreciated the present, but I also wished that I didn't have to carry it on my bike all the way from Pakistan to Ireland!

Bishop Jiwan had given us the addresses of some Christians whom we could probably stay with on our journey, and the nearest contact was at Nawabshah, a town about seventy-five miles north of Hyderabad. So a few days after our arrival in Hyderabad, we made ready to cycle there. We said goodbye to Charles, who was going to continue his journey by catching a train to Bombay.

'It's been good getting to know you over the last few days, Charles,' I said.

'Yes, we were really glad to see you that night when we had to camp at Thatta,' added John.

'I have enjoyed your company also,' replied Charles. 'It is amazing who you meet travelling on a bicycle.'

'I hope you find that quiet Indian beach you are looking for,' I said. 'You'll have no trouble getting plenty of sun, if the weather here is anything to go by!'

'And you — I hope you cycle well,' said Charles. 'It is a long way around the world, you know.'

'Yes, we know!' we said.

Then, after saying goodbye to all the Christians we had met at the compound, we set off for Nawabshah. This was a much more pleasant journey than the one through the desert from Karachi to Hyderabad, because this time we were cycling through great irrigated areas of rice, cotton and banana crops.

We arrived at the Christian quarter of Nawabshah in the late afternoon. We asked directions, and a small boy led us through the dirty, narrow, crowded streets of the town. Here and there goats idled about and great, black water-buffalo chewed the cud. The boy went through the entrance of a courtyard and soon returned in the company of a middle-aged Pakistani man.

'Hello,' said John. 'We are Christians from Ireland. We are travelling to Rahim Yar Khan. Bishop Jiwan said you might be able to help us to find somewhere to sleep.'

'Ah yes, welcome,' said the man, smiling warmly. 'My name is Samuel Gill. I am minister here. You must stay in my house.' (We found out later that his family, like quite a few others in the Indian subcontinent, had adopted British names during the colonial period.)

He ushered us into the courtyard. The house was roughly built of brick and comprised two simple bedrooms and an adjoining room, which was also used as a church. Mr Gill led us to one of the rooms.

'Please, please come,' he said, gesturing that we should enter. 'This room is for your sleeping.'

I was very touched by his ready hospitality. 'Thank you very much,' I said. 'I hope we're not putting anyone out.'

'No problem, no problem,' said Mr Gill. 'Very welcome.'

The floor of the room was hard, packed soil and the roof was made of bamboo. The door was simply a few rough boards nailed together, and there was no glass in the small windows. Occasionally small birds flew in and out of these. Our beds were typical of those in Pakistan: called *chaar pais*, they were just plain, rectangular wooden frames on legs with string stretched over them. This was the first of the many Pakistani homes in which we were to stay.

We were made to feel like honoured guests and were treated like kings. News of our arrival spread like wildfire through the Christian quarter, and soon visitors started to arrive to shake hands with us and welcome us. Later in the evening, some of the local men gathered to give us the addresses of people on whom we could call later on our journey and to offer us some advice on travelling. They were very helpful, but occasionally an argument would develop about the best way to get from one town to the next — sometimes in Urdu, sometimes in Hindi and sometimes in English. One man who was dominating the discussion insisted, 'It is better for you to cycle on the main road, not on the railway.'

I thought I had misunderstood him. I knew the Irish had a reputation for being a little unorthodox, but surely this man didn't think we would consider cycling on the railway line!

'So you think we should cycle on the road?' I asked, trying to clarify the situation.

'Yes,' replied the man, 'if you go by road to Moro, it is fifty miles. If you cycle on the railway, it is only forty-five miles, but it will be bad for the bicycles. So you must go to Moro by road, fifty miles. Understand?'

I wasn't sure I did! Perhaps sometimes people round there actually did cycle on railway lines!

The next day was Sunday, so we went to the church service held in the room next door to our own. It was a small, bare room with a rug in the middle of the floor. There was a table with a white cloth on it, behind which Mr Gill stood and led the service. There were about fifteen men, women and children present, and we all sat cross-legged and barefoot on the floor. Mr Gill started to sing a hymn in Urdu, and the others joined in. It sounded a little mournful, since there were no musical instruments to accompany the singing. Then there were some announcements in Urdu, and Mr Gill welcomed us in English. After that, there were prayers and more hymns and Mr Gill preached a sermon. The whole service lasted for about an hour. It had a slightly melancholy air to it and it seemed as if it were a ritual which the people felt they ought to go through. Sadly, the worshippers didn't seem very enthusiastic about their faith.

Then we were taken on a tour of the Christian quarter, spending a short time with each family, consuming endless cups of tea and biscuits and even some hard-boiled eggs. These very kind and lovable people lavished hospitality and sacrificial generosity upon us. At each house the whole family would come and watch us in polite fascination as we drank their tea and ate their biscuits. At times I felt as if I were an animal in the zoo! But I also felt I was in my element now, among these poor, simple people, whose values in life seemed so pure and natural compared with those of many people in the wealthy West.

Later one of the members of the church invited us to his house for a meal. Apart from the spicy food and the kindness of the host and his wife, my strongest memory of that meal is the time when a goat stuck its head between the bars of a window beside me, had a good look around the room over my shoulder, and then went about its business outside again. There was something very appealing about this lifestyle. I felt, as never before, that I was in harmony with nature.

One of the habits we were having to acquire was putting purification tablets in all our drinking water, even when we were guests in someone's home. All the drinking water was contaminated, so although the local people, who were used to it, might have sufficient antibodies in their systems to be able to cope with the bacteria, we certainly didn't. A trick we had to master was that of putting the tablets in the water without being noticed doing it — which wasn't easy, because there were often children watching us, and they're very observant. We had to be secretive about it, because our hosts might have been hurt or offended, assuming that we thought their water wasn't good enough for us.

However, our precautions with the tablets proved to be inadequate, as the next morning I awoke feeling unwell. John was feeling under the weather too. We soon came to the conclusion that we had fallen foul of our very first Asian bugs, and had contracted that most common of Third World complaints, diarrhoea. But we felt we didn't have the time to spend a few days resting in bed — we had to move on. So we said some very grateful goodbyes to the Christians of Nawabshah and set off bravely, feeling distinctly ill. Needless to say, cycling and diarrhoea are not very compatible, so we had a very difficult day's travelling. Frequently one of us would have to screech to a halt, let his bike fall to the ground with a dusty clatter and run into the nearest sugar-cane field. We tried to see the funny side of all this, but there was a serious side too, since the illness was weakening us. That day we managed to reach a small town called Moro, which the people in Nawabshah had told us about, and there we stayed with a Christian family. They persuaded us that we should rest and very kindly offered to look after us while we recovered from our illness.

Our host was a young man called Malik, who had studied medicine at Hyderabad. During the two days that we spent there Malik, John and I would sit in the living room of the house while the women busied themselves out in the courtyard, making bread or preparing the next meal. Out of modesty, the women would not come into the room when we were in there, and when it was meal-time Malik would go out and bring our food to us. An entire extended family lived there — parents, children, uncles, aunts, nephews, nieces, cousins, grandparents, grandchildren — all working together in support of one another. Each nuclear family had its own room, but everyone shared the kitchen and the toilet in the courtyard. At night we slept in Malik's room, which was chock-a-block with beds. Sometimes John and I had to dash to the toilet in the night, and we had a real problem getting past all the beds, mattresses and quilts quickly enough!

Before going to bed at night, Malik, John and I would go out for a walk past the edge of the town and out into the flat countryside. It was during these walks that some of the strongest impressions of Pakistan were indelibly imprinted upon my mind. Stepping out of that courtyard was like stepping into a world of make-believe. The ground was a soft carpet of straw and clay. As we walked through the dimly lit streets, I could hear the chink of the chains which tethered the buffaloes. They were contentedly chewing the cud, coughing occasionally. Bats flew around us — dim, fluttering shapes in the twilight. Dogs growled at us as we walked past them. We saw a man settling down for the night on his *chaar pai* outside his shop. Many other people were walking about like ghosts in the darkness, leaving the town and heading for their homes in the country, taking the dirt road that ran through the flat fields of rice. After walking for a while with them, we turned and headed back into town. People were still leaving it, walking in twos and threes or perhaps leading a donkey or a pair of bullocks pulling a cart. No one was in a hurry and there was always time for greetings. '*Assalaam alaykum*' (literally, 'Greetings in the name of the Lord'), the people would say, to which we three would reply in unison, '*Wa alaymum salaam*' ('Greetings in the name of the Lord to you too'). As we neared the town again and approached its dim lights and deep shadows, the call to prayer sounded for the last time that day from the loud-speakers on the tall minarets, which stood out darkly against the sky. The stillness of the evening was shattered for a few moments as the faithful turned their heads and their hearts towards Mecca. But for us it was merely time for bed.

On our second morning there we said farewell to Malik and his kind family and set off once again, armed with directions for getting to a Mr Jamal, the landlord of a Christian village some fifty miles away, who, Bishop Jiwan had told us, would be glad to put us up for a night or two. In the afternoon, as instructed, we stopped at a town called Kotri Kabir and went to the bank to find someone who could speak English.

John waited outside while I walked up to the counter and asked a young lady dressed in a sari, 'Do you speak English?'

'One moment,' she replied, going into one of the back rooms. She soon returned, bringing the manager with her.

'May I help you?' he asked.

'Could you please give us directions so that we can find this man?' I said, handing him the scrap of paper bearing the name and address of Mr Jamal.

'Yes, yes, I am able to help you. Please have a cup of tea with me.'

I hesitated for a moment, feeling reluctant to be delayed, but then decided that it would be best to accept the offer rather than risk offending the man. 'Thank you,' I said. 'May I bring my friend in?'

'Yes, yes. You are both very welcome.'

We were ushered into the manager's office. It was dominated by a big desk and had grubby green walls, bars on the windows and an electric fan in the ceiling. We were given tea in china cups. The manager was very interested in why we were cycling through Pakistan, so we explained the reasons behind our trip.

'You will be very welcome to stay at my house,' he said. 'We will give you good hospitality.'

'That's very kind of you, but we had planned to get to this address today,' I said, pointing to the scrap of paper. 'Mr Jamal is a friend of the Bishop of Hyderabad, whom we know.'

The manager looked a little doubtful. 'Are you sure you want to go there?' he asked. I wondered what could be wrong with the place.

'Well, I think we should stick to our plans.'

'Very well,' said the manager. 'I will get a man to go with you to show you the way.'

So after thanking the manager for his help, we set off down the national highway, following a young man on a motorbike. I couldn't wait to reach Mr Jamal's house. It had been very hot that day and many times we had been deluged with dust by buses and trucks as they strayed on to the verge of the road ahead of us. So I was looking forward to a good, cold shower.

The young man took us down the national highway for a mile or so and then turned off on to a side road, which we followed for another mile, and then on to a rough dirt track which ran through some wheat fields. After a while, the track rounded a corner and there ahead of us was a little village of mud-brick houses with thatch-and-mud roofs. There was no sign here of a big landlord's house. I could only conclude that Mr Jamal was, in fact, only slightly better off than the rest of the inhabitants of this very poor village. I wondered how we would cope in such primitive conditions. But there was no way we could turn back now, because the children of the village had already seen us and so had some of the adults. What on earth would these poor people make of us? There was nothing for it but to go and meet them.

The noise of the motorbike heralded our arrival, and soon lots of curious and uninhibited children came running to see the two Westerners and their strange, overloaded bikes. The adults also stopped what they were doing and stared in our direction as we waited at the edge of the village. Eventually a young man wearing traditional clothes and sandals came up to us. He looked intelligent but slightly worried. Evidently he was wondering what on earth we could want at their village. He spoke in Urdu to the man who had led us there. I didn't know what they were saying, but I was very keen to make a friendly gesture, so I spoke directly to the young man.

'Do you speak English?' I asked.

He hesitated, trying to think of the right word, then replied, 'Little.'

'We are Christians,' I informed him. 'Bishop Jiwan of Hyderabad sends us here. We come to see Mr Jamal.'

He must have understood me, because he began to relax. He spoke again to the man with the motorbike, who then started his engine. John and I shook hands with him and thanked him with a '*Shukryia*'. He then set off in a cloud of dust.

The young man now turned to us, shook our hands and said, 'Welcome! Name Walter.'

'My name John,' I replied. 'This John too.' I gestured towards my travelling companion.

'Come,' said Walter and led us into the village.

It was about the size of a football pitch and had a ten-foot-high wall along three sides. Another wall ran across the centre of the village and little mud houses were built on to it on both sides of its length. Parallel to this central wall were two exterior walls against which the animals' outhouses had been built. Just outside the village stood a camel under a tree, grabbing some leaves with its thick, rubbery lips. It swung its head round on its long neck to watch us as we passed. At the village entrance, two harnessed buffaloes were patiently walking around in a circle, operating a metal wheel which was cutting up grass and chaff. All over the village between the houses and the outhouses buffaloes lay about, lazily chewing their cuds, and goats with short, white hair and long ears strutted about gracefully while their kids chased and played with one another. Here a dog lay sleeping in the sun, there a young boy sat on a small stool, milking a cow. The women sat in their colourful saris in little groups outside their houses, cooking food and baking *chapattis* in mud ovens.

We wheeled our bikes into the village and leaned them against a wall while someone went to get Mr Jamal. The women moved cautiously away from us, despite our attempts to put them at their ease with numerous smiles and '*Salaams*'. Two chairs were brought out for us and we sat in the sun and waited. In the meantime Mr Jamal's son, Parvez, arrived. He could speak some English, so the four of us sat talking and drinking some rather milky, stewed tea out of china cups. As we sat there, it struck me that though the conditions were primitive, there was something attractive about such a simple, natural way of life.

Eventually Mr Jamal arrived from the fields. He was a tall, thin man with receding hair and a grey beard and was wearing the baggy, off-white clothes which were normal for Pakistani men. He looked a little concerned when he saw us. He must have been wondering what on earth two Westerners like us could want in his village.

We smiled and shook his hand. 'We are Christians from Ireland,' I said. 'Bishop Jiwan has sent us to you.' Parvez translated what we had said for his father. Mr

Jamal nodded and looked a little relieved, then said something in Urdu to his son.

'My father says he knows Bishop Jiwan,' said Parvez. 'He comes here once a year. Father says you are both very welcome to stay in our village. It is an honour to have you as guests.'

As we continued talking with Mr Jamal, Parvez and Walter, we learned quite a good deal about the village. Mr Jamal was the head of the community, which comprised about 120 people. The village had no electricity, and its drinking water had to be carried from a nearby well. The fields were irrigated by a system of channels supplied by large canals which watered the whole countryside. In a good year the village was virtually self-sufficient in wheat, rice, sugar and bananas, and often they were able to sell the surplus at the local market and earn some cash. That money would perhaps pay for some other food-stuff that they were short of, or it might buy some medicine for the sick. However, in a bad year, when the rains either failed to come or came too heavily and caused flooding, the margin separating the village from a desperate fight for survival was quickly narrowed.

There were a number of sick people in the village, and Mr Jamal took us to meet some of them. One little baby with a hare-lip was seriously ill and coughed and sneezed continually. He was expected to die soon. Children frequently died of malnourishment, since their starved bodies were not strong enough to cope with the many common diseases, some of them caused by unhygienic conditions. However, if a child made it to the age of five, then he had a good chance of surviving.

I noticed that despite the poverty, there was a strong communal solidarity, and that the sick were lovingly cared for. One old man was completely blind and had been so from birth. However, he was not left in a corner somewhere and forgotten, as so many of the old and sick are in the so-called 'Christian' West, but, rather, he was an important member of that community. He accompanied Walter, Parvez, John and I as we walked around the village.

We were shown the village's animals, a vital part of the community's livelihood. The male buffaloes worked on treadmills to operate simple machines like that used to crush the syrup out of sugar-cane, while the females provided a rich milk that was made into curd. The goats also gave milk, and the chickens provided eggs and meat. The villagers kept bees too; children would limber up into the trees where the hives were to collect honey.

We wandered out among the fields that surrounded the village and along the small, hardened ditches that separated the rice from the wheat. The blind man chattered away in Punjabi, but he also knew a few words of textbook English.

'What is your name?' he asked me.

'My name is John,' I replied.

This use of his schoolboy English pleased him immensely and he laughed heartily. Then he continued, 'My name is Afrim,' and again chuckled like a child.

We turned and began to make our way back along the dusty ditch that led to the village. There was silence for a while and then the blind man, thinking up some more English, broke the silence:

'I want to see,' he said, but this time he didn't laugh.

When we got back, it was time for the evening meal in Walter's house. We stepped into the dimness of the mud building and sat on a *chaar pai*. There was little else in the room, apart from some chests where clothes and other valuables were kept away from the rats. I heard something moving about in the thatch of the roof above me. 'Maybe it's a rat or a lizard!' I thought, remembering our unpleasant encounter with the lizard in Karachi.

As long as whatever it was stayed in the roof, I wouldn't mind too much, but I didn't cherish the thought of some loathsome little creature landing on my head and running down my back!

Soon Walter came in with food on a tray. 'This is *chapatti* made from wheat grown here,' he said, pointing to some round, flat, wafer-thin pieces of bread. 'The women make it each day.

'This is spinach,' he continued, gesturing to a bowl of dark green cabbage-like vegetable, 'and these are mustard leaves.'

Most people in Pakistan eat with their hands, and since this village had probably never had a foreign visitor before and so had no knives and forks, John and I resolved to do in Pakistan as the Pakistanis do. The locals were adept at eating in this manner, gathering up a small portion of rice with the four fingers of the right hand, kneading it into a sticky lump, dipping it into chilli sauce and then scooping it mouthwards. John and I found that it wasn't quite as easy as it looked! But since we had to do it, we got the hang of it in the end.

The mustard leaves made the meal very hot. It wasn't particularly hot by Pakistani standards, but even after several weeks of trying to become accustomed to the new diet, we were still having problems stomaching it. So we were greatly relieved when Walter brought in some buffalo curd. Normally I'm not too partial to sour milk or raw yoghurt, but when you feel as if you've just swallowed a shovelful of red-hot coals, some buffalo curd is very welcome indeed!

We were very conscious that these simple people were lavishing on us all the kindness and sacrificial hospitality that they could muster. I felt privileged to share their beautifully simple living and their oneness with the natural environment. Equally, they felt honoured that we had come to visit them and, indeed, were so pleased by our visit that that night Mr Jamal called together a meeting of the Christian men at one of the houses, so that we could tell them all more about ourselves: who we were, where we were from and what we were doing. As they entered everyone took their shoes off and left them at the door, and sat cross-legged on cane mats on the earthen floor of the mud hut.

Someone opened the meeting with a prayer and everyone (except us) sang two hymns. Invited to speak, John told how he had become a Christian. Then I also gave my testimony and went on to tell them why we were cycling around the world and how we hoped to raise money in Northern Ireland for work among the refugees in Thailand. However, the translation, carried out by Walter, was not altogether accurate, because we later discovered that the men thought we were trying to raise money in Pakistan. I was deeply moved when the men, despite their poverty, tried to give us some rupees for the refugees, such was the sincerity of their Christian love and commitment. Of course, we had to refuse the money, because these people desperately needed it themselves.

I was profoundly challenged by the sacrifice they had been willing to make. Even though some of their own children were very ill and urgently needed costly medical attention, these people were still prepared to look to the needs of others — even those of people in a distant country. With shame, I thought of my own skimpy giving to God's work, and that from a situation of relative plenty. I remembered that in order to get a visa to enter the USA, we had been obliged to promise not to attempt to raise any money there. And here were these poor people, just existing at subsistence level, with virtually nothing in the world, and they were prepared to give away what little they had so that others could have a better life.

I prayed silently at the time: 'Lord, we Christians in the West have really got our priorities wrong. We get so caught up and absorbed by our own selfish concerns, building our petty empires of material possessions. We're too concerned with things like houses, mortgages, interest rates, cars, clothes, cameras, pop stars, music . . . Let these simple, innocent servants of yours teach us something about real Christianity. Help us, too, to put you first, and then to love our neighbours as ourselves.'

It was then time for bed, and one of the men led us across the village to the little mud hut in which we were to spend the night. It was a very simple dwelling: there was a doorway but no door, and a hole in the wall but no window. We leaned our bikes against one of the walls and then rolled out our sleeping bags on the *chaar pais* and crawled in, while the man, who was to spend the night with us in case we had any problems, occupied a third bed.

In the dancing candle-light I could see a dog curled up and asleep in one corner of the room. Something was moving about in a pile of straw near my bed. And then there were the lizards on the walls, which occasionally darted this way and that in pursuit of mosquitoes and other insect prey. Up in the roof, something was rustling the thatch. I hoped it was a hen and not a snake.

The candle was snuffed out, but in the starlit near-darkness outside I could still make out the shapes of the houses and the dozing buffaloes. It was so simple, yet so beautiful. I closed my eyes and thanked God for bringing me here, for allowing me to meet these people, for the sights and sounds of his creation. Outside a nearby buffalo made itself comfortable on the ground, grunting contentedly. All the while the crickets in the fields kept up their relentless, high-pitched chirping. It was warm, and the night hummed.

It took me quite a while to get to sleep, because of the noises made by the animals both inside and outside the hut. But I didn't mind this, since I wanted some time to myself to think about the new and fascinating experience of living in such a simple community, right next to nature. I reflected that although there was much to be said for such a lifestyle, there was also a less attractive side to the coin. In many ways these people led very hard and difficult lives. They had to cope with disease, dysentery and hard work in the heat. They were obliged to walk quite some distance to fetch water. They also had to live with continual uncertainty, wondering whether there would be enough rain to make their crops grow.

Next morning, instead of being awakened by an alarm-clock, we were aroused by a little buffalo calf which had happened to wander into our hut. It was promptly chased out by the man who had spent the night with us. Then Walter came into the hut and greeted us. He suggested that if we wanted to urinate, we should do so out in the fields, since there was nowhere else to do it! We were rather embarrassed by this, and told him we could wait.

We rose to meet the new day. After we had eaten a breakfast of *chapatti* bread, buffalo curd and tea with Mr Jamal, Walter and Parvez took us to see the sugar-canes being crushed. In a small field beside the village two buffalo were pulling a rotating wooden shaft which powered a simple machine of metal wheels rolling against each other. Walter sat at the machine and fed a sugar-cane into it, while the juice which had been squeezed out of it by the wheels dripped into a bucket below. Then Walter folded the cane in half and fed it through the machine again, then folded it once more and fed it through a third time, so that every last drop of juice was extracted. Once a number of canes had received this treatment, the bucketful of juice was emptied into a large forty-gallon drum at the side of the field. The juice was dark brown and sticky and had a few flies and some other foreign bodies floating on its surface. The community would then sell this syrup in order to earn much-needed cash.

Though we were loath to do it, we had to leave the village behind us that day, since we had to move on in order to get to Rahim Yar Khan for Christmas. It was hard to say goodbye to such a haven of peace, kindness and hospitality. In those all-too-short eighteen hours we had spent there, we had made many friends, and parted from them regretfully with many handshakes and '*Shukryias*'. As we set off, I reflected on the many lessons about living I had learned there, and began to look forward to the many other stimulating experiences that lay ahead and to the many other kind people we would meet on our travels.

That day we pressed on north to the city of Sukkur, where with some help from the local people we found the Zanana Christian Hospital, which was run by John and Heather McCormick, two missionaries from Scotland. They were another link in that chain of Christian contacts which kept extending as we travelled through Pakistan. John came out to see us at the gate of the Hospital and, once we had introduced ourselves, warmly invited us to stay at his house and took us to meet his wife. After we had had a thorough wash (which we badly needed, as there hadn't been any opportunity to wash at the Christian village!), Heather treated us to a wonderful meal of eggs, chips, apple flan and tea — a refreshingly British repast after all the highly spiced Pakistani food we had been eating on our travels. John and Heather asked us about our experiences on our trip so far and we enquired about their work at the Hospital.

'Well, I must admit that we're in a rather frustrating situation here,' said John. 'To tell the truth, the Hospital isn't operating at the moment.'

'I'd wondered if that was the case,' I said. 'I've noticed that there aren't many people about.'

'That's right,' said John. 'There aren't any patients here at all, though we could cater for hundreds. And the reason why we're closed is that we don't have enough Christian staff to run the Hospital.'

'Are you talking about nationals or expatriate Christians?' asked John Rodgers.

'Both,' replied Heather. 'There aren't that many Pakistani Christians to start with, so we need workers from overseas. It's such a pity that there aren't more medics and nurses coming out here from the West.'

'Yes, it's a great shame,' said John sadly. 'Here's a fully equipped hospital, here's an open mission field — but there are no labourers to bring in the harvest.'

We lingered with the McCormicks for a few hours the next day, because they seemed as glad of our company as we were of theirs. They were obviously lonely and depressed by the difficult situation they were in. Regretfully, we said goodbye to them that morning and made for a town called Ghotki, stopping on the way to sit down beside a canal and eat the sandwiches with which we had been supplied.

We arrived at Ghotki in the late afternoon and stayed the night with Roger Pomeroy, an English missionary working with the Revd Hidayat Masih (another of our contacts), who was the pastor of a Protestant church in the town. Roger was working for the International Christian Fellowship and was involved in evangelism among the local tribal people. It so happened that the day on which we arrived was the birthday of Roger's five-year-old daughter, and we were invited to her party, despite being a little over-aged! It was an enjoyable if slightly odd experience to be among all the fun of a British child's birthday party — complete with cake, candles, fizzy drinks, sweets, peanuts and games — while in the street outside were all the noises and sights typical of an Asian city.

The next day we were eager to get on to Rahim Yar Khan so that we could spend Christmas with Lily Givans, who was expecting us, so we set off early in the morning. In the late afternoon, we arrived at the boys' hostel in Rahim Yar Khan where Lily worked, guided there by the map which Roger Pomeroy had drawn for us. As we entered the courtyard of the hostel, a boy ran off shouting, '*Anglaisia! Anglaisia*!' Lily, Maureen (a missionary from England) and the boys were having a party at the time, and all of them came charging out to greet us. '*Assalaam alaykum*!' they shouted. 'Welcome to Rahim Yar Khan!' The boys swarmed around us like bees in a hive, excited about our arrival and fascinated by our bicycles.

'Well, well,' said Lily, smiling broadly. 'You've made it here! Well done!' A middle-aged lady who looked much younger than her years, Lily had brown hair and was dressed like a Pakistani woman, with a long, green, patterned top and plain, baggy trousers. I was so pleased to see her that I just wanted to give her a big hug, but for some reason she seemed a little bit standoffish, and didn't shake our hands or even come near to us. I wondered anxiously if perhaps we were somehow an embarrassment to her. Maybe we weren't really too welcome here.

'Thanks, Lily,' said John in reply to her greeting. 'It's really good to see you. It seems a long time since we last saw you back home in Dungannon.'

'We've been looking forward to getting here for a long time,' I said. 'It's great to be here — just great!'

'We've been waiting for this for a long time too, haven't we, Maureen?' said Lily. 'By the way, this is Maureen Hider, who works with me here at the hostel.'

We exchanged helloes.

'Where have you come from today?' asked Lily.

'We stayed last night with the Pomeroys in Ghotki,' I replied. 'Roger drew us a little map to get us here to the hostel, so we were able to cycle straight here without getting lost.'

'All the way from Ghotki?' said Maureen in surprise. 'That's a long way in one day!'

'Well, we've got used to that sort of pace by now,' I said. 'But we're really looking forward to getting a few days of rest here!'

John was looking around him with interest. 'So this is the hostel we've been hearing so much about back home,' he commented.

'Yes, this is it,' said Lily. 'Maybe it doesn't look much, but it's home for all these kids. Come with me and I'll show you around the place.'

After only hearing and reading about Lily's work for years, it was exciting to actually see it for myself. The hostel (which also served as a school) was small and was substantially if roughly built of brick. It had two floors and a water tank on top. Upstairs were the boys' dormitories, while downstairs were the classrooms and the kitchen.

We also met some of the fortunate children who were getting a good start in life there. Some of them were a little shy, but most seemed happy and full of life, with twinkling brown eyes, white teeth and big smiles. A few of them had rather thin legs and none of them were exactly overweight, but they all looked healthy enough.

'So where do these kids come from?' asked John.

'They're all from the Marwari villages round about,' answered Lily. 'The Marwari are the tribal group in this area. Each boy has at least one Christian parent. The parents pay a nominal fee for the boys' schooling, while the rest of the cost is covered by our missionary society, the International Christian Fellowship. The parents are very keen to send their boys here, as they get a good education with plenty of Christian teaching, and they're also sure to get a good diet.'

'So what do you and Maureen do at the school?' I asked.

'We're mostly involved with the boys' Christian education. We're also working with the local women, running Bible studies and evangelistic classes here in the town and in the outlying villages. So we're pretty busy, as you can imagine!'

Then Lily and Maureen were taken to their nearby home in a horse-drawn tonga, and we followed on our bikes. The house was one of an avenue of fine homes, all of them built with surrounding walls and iron gates at the front. Their house was really a small annexe built on to the gable wall of a larger house owned by a rich businessman.

Once we were inside the house, Lily said, 'Look, I'm sorry I didn't give you two chaps a good, Irish handshake or seem over-pleased to see you when we met at the hostel. But, you see, this is a Muslim country, and here it's considered very bad manners for men and women to touch one another in public. To keep our credibility here we have to observe the cultural taboos. I do hope you understand.'

I felt greatly relieved by this explanation. 'Oh, yes, of course we understand,' I assured her. 'We wouldn't want to do anything to undermine your work here.'

John and I had cycled eighty miles that day and we had frequently been squeezed off the road by hurtling buses and trucks, so it was very pleasant to have a friendly home to come to that evening and to be able to enjoy a cold shower and some familiar food. Shortly after arriving, we were both presented with a bundle of letters and Christmas cards from family and friends, and so our first evening there was spent gleaning all the news from home. We were pleased that certain supplies we had been expecting had arrived, such as vitamin pills, water purification tablets and the foam padding for our handlebars, but we were also worried because our spare tyres hadn't turned up yet.

During our stay at Rahim Yar Khan, we slept on two *chaar pais* in the office of a nearby school that was closed down for the Christmas holidays. In Muslim Pakistan, it was very important that John and I did not sleep in the same house as two single women. Missionaries always have to be careful to avoid damaging their ministry by behaviour which, however innocent it might really be, would be misunderstood by the local people.

We spent a very enjoyable Christmas with Lily, relaxing our bodies and minds after the strain of the past few months, recovering from our illness, enjoying some Irish banter, playing Scrabble and reading *National Geographic* magazines. We also gave our bikes a thorough servicing, did some painting in Lily's house, and, best of all, ate sumptuously. Lily and Maureen had been saving up goodies for a long time, so that we could enjoy them too. We were also invited to a number of parties given by the other missionaries.

The four of us played some highly competitive games of Scrabble. Lily was a very accomplished player — so accomplished, in fact, that she was beating us hands down every time. So while she was out of the room in the middle of one game, John, Maureen and I hatched a devious conspiracy against her.

'Look, there's no way any one of us is going to beat Lily,' I said. 'Let's work together, and see if we can't beat her!'

And so on the understanding that we would confess to our scandalous behaviour at the end of the game, we continued playing, passing useful letters to one another under the table! But it was to no avail, because Lily still won, even with us cheating. It just goes to show that crime doesn't pay.

All this fun helped to make the separation from home a little easier for us over the Christmas period, when we were thinking very much of our families and of all the parties and get-togethers they would be having. Both John and I phoned home from Rahim Yar Khan, which cheered both us and our families. Our thoughts of distant Ireland were particularly strong on Christmas Day itself, and since we knew we were roughly five hours ahead of our people at home, we could calculate what they would be doing at any particular time.

There would be no Christmas presents for us this year — or so we thought, until on Christmas morning we found about a dozen little packages for us around the Christmas tree from Lily and Maureen. They contained delightful things like Pocket Mastermind, packets of soup, key-rings and other souvenirs of Pakistan, a spelling game, teabags, milk-shakes — all the sort of things that would make life that little bit more pleasant for us on our travels over the next few months. We appreciated these gifts especially, because we knew they had been sent out for Lily and Maureen themselves.

Later in the morning, we went to the local church for the Christmas service. A modern brick building, plastered on the inside and well finished, the church had been paid for by a rich Canadian businessman and was part of an all-purpose Christian centre which was used for lay training courses, pastors' retreats and Bible weeks. There were three pairs of electric fans in the ceiling, although they were not then working, since this was the winter and it was cool by Pakistani standards. As it was Christmas, multicoloured streamers had been hung across the ceiling and over the doors. There were also lots of very colourful and cheery balloons decorating the church.

At the doors were two piles of shoes — one the men's, one the women's. Everyone sat cross-legged on red, blue and brown cotton mats on the smooth concrete floor — the men on one side of the church, the women on the other. The service was conducted from a low platform at the front. On its left side was the Communion table and on the right was the reading-desk. Each was draped with a white cloth on which a cross stood out boldly. In the servic there was a good deal of lively singing and clapping, accompanied by hand drums and a hand-bellow portable organ. There were also Scripture readings, prayers, an offering and a sermon. It was all very informal. During the proceedings people frequently came in or got up and went out; there were children crying and babies were being breast-fed right among the congregation.

Afterwards we sat out on the church's lawn with the other missionaries and the Pakistani church members and ate our Christmas dinner together. This was not the sort of festive meal John and I were used to, though: there was no turkey or ham or cranberry sauce. There was no plum-pudding or ginger beer or Brussels sprouts. Instead, we had a typically Pakistani repast: goat meat and curried rice. And to wash this down we had ice-cold boiled water. This wasn't the most sumptuous of meals by Western standards, but it was the best these people could afford, and so we appreciated it.

On Boxing Day we hired two great, big, black bicycles in the bazaar (we were giving our own machines thorough overhauls during our stay at Rahim Yar Khan, so they weren't usable at that time) and headed out with John Rana, a Pakistani Christian, to visit one of the

Marwari villages. The vast majority of the people in Pakistan were Muslims, but the Marwari were an exception, being a low-caste Hindu tribe with close ties with similar tribes in India. They didn't mix freely with other Pakistanis and had their own distinctive customs and dialect. Lily and the other missionaries connected with the hostel worked among them, preaching the gospel and training the people in Christian discipleship. In this particular village, a small fellowship group — the beginnings of a church — had been formed.

We were introduced to the chief of the community and were given tea. As we were shown round the village, I noticed that the children had only the most ragged of clothes, and one little boy we saw had none at all. Flies were crawling over his face and body. The men were dressed just like other Pakistanis in baggy, off-white shirts and trousers, although their headgear was unusual. Some of them wore loose scarves over their heads and shoulders, while others wore turbans of white, twisted towel. I thought the village was generally less tidy than the Christian community we had stayed at, and some of the houses seemed to be falling apart.

A number of cottage industries were flourishing in the village, perhaps because it was fairly near a town, where there would be a market for manufactured goods. We were taken to see some cobblers at work. Half a dozen men were sitting on the ground in a doorway working away with sharp metal awls, small knives, pots of glue and pieces of leather. Scattered about were numerous pairs of slipper-like sandals in varying degrees of completion. The men seemed flattered that we wanted to watch them at their work, and with pride they showed us finished examples of their craft.

One little old man with a bloodshot and cataract eye took us to see the house of the local god. He rang a bell to let the god know we were coming and we all had to take our shoes off and stoop down to pass through the small doorway of the little coloured brick hut. Inside there were pictures of the monkey-god and a smell of incense, which was supposed to placate him. Outside we saw a young man praying and bowing down to a tablet of stone placed under a tree. I found this all very interesting and was struck by the thought that man, throughout history and in every culture, in various ways and using different rituals and symbols, has expressed a tendency to look up to a higher being. He seems to have a need to believe in some all-powerful, all-seeing entity — or entities — which control the weather and many other aspects of the daily life of the individual and the community. All over the world people are looking for God. All the more reason, therefore, for Christians to spread the news that God has already revealed himself in the Person of Jesus Christ.

While staying at Rahim Yar Khan, we talked to a number of missionary workers and Pakistani nationals and heard some thought-provoking comments on the adverse effects of Muslim belief and culture. In Islam women are very much second-class citizens and are regarded more as chattels or objects to be owned rather than human beings. One missionary doctor we met told us about the prevailing male chauvinism: 'If a mother gives birth to a girl, she cries with anguish and shame. If a wife does not bear a son, she may be divorced by her husband. I know of one man who married and divorced seven wives because none of them was able to bear him any children. He blamed them for being infertile, and in his blind arrogance never considered the possibility that he himself might be the one who was infertile.'

Another missionary we talked to told us about Pakistan's endemic bureaucratic inefficiency and corruption: 'I'm afraid the aid given by foreign governments through official channels sometimes gets squandered by the authorities and merely goes to line the pockets of the bureaucrats. Personally, I believe that aid administered through independent agencies like Tear Fund, who have responsible people actually on the ground in the field, is a much more effective means of ministry in real terms.'

We also heard the same thing from Pakistani nationals. While in the Sind Desert, we heard how government money was absorbed by layer upon layer of bureaucracy, so that in the end there was little if any money left for anything actually to be done to improve conditions for the people who were meant to benefit from it.

Another cause for concern among Christians in Pakistan was the revival of militant Islam following the Islamic Revolution in Iran, which had sent reverberations throughout the Muslim world. We heard about a Church of Pakistan minister who had been threatened with death by Muslim mullahs unless he stopped broadcasting Christian worship over loudspeakers on Sundays.

However, despite these wrongs in Muslim culture, I had to admit that there must be plenty in our own Western culture which an outsider could rightly criticise. Also, on a personal level, the Muslim people we met on our travels were kind and hospitable to us, and it has to be said that their prayerful devotion to Allah could teach us Christians a thing or two. Unlike the Muslims, we have real, personal access to God the Father in our prayers through his Son, and yet we fail to pray even as much as the Muslims do. Really we should want to pray more than they do! Also, Muslim morality has things to recommend it. For example, Muslim women are taught to cover their bodies, to dress modestly and not to flaunt themselves in front of men.

On 30th December, the day before we planned to

move on, we breathed a sigh of relief when our spare tyres arrived from home. They had been posted by my mother on 21st October! We would certainly need them, as at this stage we were still using the tyres on which we had left Ireland. John decided to change his tyres there and then, but I chose to leave my old tyres on until they were worn right through.

And so on the last day of the year, we said goodbye to Lily, Maureen, the other missionaries and the national Christians, thanking them for the time we had spent with them, and so set off on our gleaming, newly serviced bicyles, heading north-east towards Lahore, on our way to India.

Our next port of call was the town of Bahawalpur, where we hoped to stay one night with the family of Pastor Umar Masih, whom we had met at Rahimyar Khan. When we arrived, we were shocked to hear from his American wife that Mr Masih was in hospital, having suffered an attack of angina the previous night. So after a wash and a cup of tea, we went to see him in hospital. He was lying in an iron-framed bed in a crowded, grubby ward. He was still feeling weak, but was in less pain now. Mrs Masih had brought her husband his evening meal in three steel dishes. It was normal for relatives to feed the patients. Those who lived out of town would even stay at the hospital, perhaps sleeping under the patient's bed.

We spent the night at the home of the Masihs, and in the morning had breakfast with the Gulzers, one of the more wealthy families in Mr Masih's church. Mr Gulzer was an English teacher and his three daughters and one son were all medical students! They were very interested in us and our round-the-world trip and treated us to a lavish breakfast of eggs, toast, buffalo butter, jam, *kebabs*, coconut, rice and tea.

Fortified and cheered by this latest expression of

Pakistani kindness and hospitality, we set off in high spirits towards the city of Multan, which lay about sixty miles north of Bahawalpur. But our exuberance was to be short-lived, because as we were nearing the bridge over the River Sutlej, disaster struck. An ominous crack issued from the rear of my bicycle. Dreading what I might find, I glanced behind me and saw to my horror that the wheel had developed a wobble! I leapt off my bike and anxiously inspected the damage. One of the spokes had broken — the first spoke to fail us on the expedition so far. I had plenty of spare spokes in my saddle-bag, so I decided to replace the broken one when we arrived in Multan. However, once we got there and I tried to carry out the repair, I realised that unfortunately the spoke happened to be on the same side of the wheel as the sprocket-block (the component which contains the gears and upon which the chain sits). So in order to replace the spoke, I would have to remove the sprocket-block. But I then discovered that I couldn't remove it. When I applied the block-remover to the block, the metal of both mushed together like cheese against a grater. This was not very surprising, since the block had borne a load of sixteen stone up some very steep gradients and so had become 'welded' on to the wheel by sheer pressure. In the end, I had to take the wheel to a workshop, where an 'engineer' at once reached for an enormous hammer and started bashing the sprocket-block! With horror, I watched the scene of destruction which now unfolded before my eyes. I wondered if the wheel could possibly survive this 'repair' job. By hook and by crook, the workman managed to replace the broken spoke and welded the block back together again. This piece of work didn't cost too much in terms of money, but it cost me dearly in terms of anxiety! And to make matters worse, I knew that this hatchet job would bring only temporary respite, because what would happen when the next spoke broke? Then the whole block would have to be replaced, since it wouldn't be able to stand a second hammering. And, although we had many spare parts, a sprocket-block wasn't among them. It looked as if a crisis lay ahead!

That wasn't the only crisis I had to face, though. Romance was in the air! One evening we pulled into a small town to stay with a Christian family overnight and spent our time with a young man named Buta, who was a student at Hyderabad and was at home for a few days when we called. Both John and I were suffering from the last meal of hot curry and rice we had eaten. Buta called the local nurse round to see us. Some time later she arrived: a lovely, slim, black-haired woman with very beautiful eyes named Jameela. After giving us some tablets and telling us to stay off the chillies, she accepted an invitation to stay on for tea. During tea, Jameela and Buta exchanged words in Urdu and started laughing, looking at John and me.

'What are you talking about?' I asked, wanting to know what the joke was.

They laughed again, and seemed reluctant to tell me what was so funny.

'Buta, what are you laughing about?' I persisted.

'Very well, I will tell you,' he said with amusement. 'Jameela says that your name sounds like the Urdu name "Jan", which means "beloved one".'

We all laughed at this and continued to chat, but from the way Jameela kept smiling at me, I started to get the distinct impression that she hadn't been altogether joking in what she had said.

Later she remarked to me, 'I would like to be coming to Ireland,' and then I really began to get hot under the collar! All my alarm-bells started ringing. I know the Pakistanis believe in arranged marriages, but this little arrangement was happening just a bit too fast for me!

The next day Jameela telephoned, wanting to speak to me. 'How is your sickness today, John?' she asked. 'Are you feeling better?'

'Oh yes, a lot better, thanks,' I replied, guessing that she was interested in more than my present health.

'You will be leaving soon?' the Pakistani beauty enquired.

'Er — yes — soon. Very soon!'

'Are you married?'

Oh, no! Here it comes, I thought. 'No. I'm not married,' I replied, getting more uncomfortable by the second and wishing that some natural disaster like an earthquake or a tornado would swallow me up and get me out of this tight corner. My hands were sweaty now and the phone felt slippery.

'Do you have a girlfriend in Ireland?' asked Jameela, bulldozing her way along, while I timidly suffered.

'Yes — yes — lots!' I replied, allowing myself to adopt a rather liberal interpretation of the word 'girlfriend' in these drastic circumstances.

'Do you like me?' continued Jameela, undaunted by my reticence. This was true torture!

I suppose an honest answer would have been: 'Yes, I like the look of you, but I don't like your pushiness!' But fortunately I didn't have to make any answer, because just then Buta interrupted us to say that his mother had to make an urgent phone call, and asked Jameela to phone back in ten minutes.

Buta's mother then made her call, while I revealed to John and Buta the embarrassing nature of the conversation I had just had with Jameela. They were amazed and amused at the same time.

'What on earth are you going to do when she rings back?' asked John.

I thought for a panicky moment. 'I know!' I said.

'Buta, when the phone rings, I'll run like a scalded cat to the loo, and you tell her where I am and that I'm indisposed at that moment. I don't want to hurt her feelings, but maybe this will start to get the message across that I don't want to marry her!'

'Do you want me to ask her not to ring back?' asked Buta.

'Maybe you could do that,' I said, 'but it might be better to deflate her hopes a little more gently. So if she rings back a second time — '

Suddenly the phone burst into life! In a flash, I got out of the room, ran past the puzzled women outside in the courtyard and made for the toilet. But there was someone in there! So I rushed out of the courtyard into the street, where I tried to look relaxed and casual, but realised that in a blue pullover and trousers, I must stick out like a sore thumb. I felt like the dunce in a classroom, standing alone in a corner. Despite my predicament, I couldn't help being amused by this latest addition to my experience of the rich tapestry of life! I wondered just what the women in the courtyard had thought of my extremely urgent desire to get to the toilet, and then my mad dash into the street after I found it was engaged. And what had the people in the street thought of the crazy Westerner who had rushed out into the street looking panic-stricken, and then stood about trying to be unobtrusive?

Soon Buta and John came out. 'Jameela's coming round to see you,' John informed me with a broad grin on his face.

'What?' I cried. 'You've got to be joking! I think I'll go for a long walk. Buta, take me to see the Indus — I want to see the river. Let's get out of here!'

Buta and John laughed, apparently unmoved by my plight. 'No, we're only joking,' Buta assured me. 'When my mother saw you running outside, she came in and told Jameela to stop ringing here. She said that if she wanted to see you, she should come round here.'

'Oh no!' I said. 'So she is coming round! Come on — let's get out of here — up the road, anywhere!'

Buta laughed again. 'No, no. Don't worry. Jameela won't come round — not when Mama is cross.'

The next morning we got up with the Muslims' first call to prayer, ate a hasty breakfast, said goodbye to Buta and then beat a fast retreat. We cycled for three solid hours without looking round. I had escaped!

And so we pressed on towards India, on the way visiting Harappa Road and the excavations of the remains of the civilisation which had flourished there at around 5,000 BC. At Lahore, on the border, we visited Badshahi, the world's largest mosque, and there made preparations to say goodbye to Pakistan. Many kind people had helped us to enjoy their country and culture and to teach us a little more about life in general. So we wrote a letter to each person we had stayed with or who had helped us in any way and enclosed a gift for any whom we had been unable to pay. We had spent an amazing six weeks in our first Third World country.

This was a time not only for looking back but also for looking forward, for just seventeen miles down the road lay India, the greatest democracy in the world and, with its 700 million people, the world's second most populous country. India: a land of diverse Hindu religions, of rich history and culture, of great wealth and appalling poverty.

5
North India

At the border crossing at Wagah, we passed through the Pakistani customs without incident, then walked our bikes a short distance along the road to the point where a white line marked the exact location of the border with India. It was very quiet there and no vehicles were crossing the line. However, large quantities of goods were crossing the border, carried in wooden boxes on the heads of Pakistani men and handed over at the white line, under close supervision, to Indian men, who carried the boxes on.

With a sense of doing something momentous, we stepped over the line into India. On the right-hand side of the road, two men sat at a little table. Although they wore a uniform similar to that of the Pakistani border guards, unlike them they had beards and wore turbans on their heads.

'Please be coming here and please be showing me passports,' said one of the men. 'Ah, British!' he said with evident friendliness as he glanced at our documents. 'Be very welcome in India.'

The other official was showing no interest in our passports, but was becoming increasingly enthralled by our mode of transport.

'You are coming all the way from England by bicycle?' he enquired with amazement.

'Yes, all the way, although we flew between Athens and Karachi,' I replied, feeling proud of our achievement.

'It is not possible!' exclaimed the man. 'Please be telling me how you did this!'

And so we told the story of our travels, and this helped to break the ice as we went through the immigration control, health checks and customs. At customs, the bikes and our valuables were noted down on our passports, to ensure that we would take them out of the country again. The officials' interest in our bikes speeded things up for us so much that the entire border crossing took us only seventy-five minutes, whereas we had been warned beforehand that it might take several hours.

Having entered India, we cycled for a short distance down a pleasant tree-lined road and then stopped for our lunch of peanut butter and bread. As we sat under a tree, some young women wearing brightly coloured saris passed through the nearby fields. Unlike the women of Pakistan, their arms and heads were not covered. On seeing us they pointed, laughed and giggled. This relaxed behaviour was quite a change from the atmosphere in Pakistan, where the women were rather oppressed, and dared not look at a man. The Indian men dressed more casually too, and loose cotton shirts and trousers were the usual attire. Because the religion of the Indian Punjab is Sikhism, many of the men wore turbans. The young Sikh boys were a remarkable sight, since they wore their hair in buns on the top of their heads, often with a white cloth placed tightly over it.

We cycled on through the Indian countryside. The land was flat and very fertile, thanks to irrigation channels which carried water from the rivers. The road from the border, which was raised up six or seven feet above the level of the surrounding fields, was straight but rather bumpy. Perhaps this was because it was considered to be a route of only minor importance, since there was little traffic across the border. Generally the roads in India were on a par with those in Pakistan. All along the road were electric pylons and telegraph-poles (some of them not quite vertical!) bearing many wires. In the border area, we also saw a number of military barracks and a lot of well equipped soldiers. I found it offensive that both India and Pakistan were willing to maintain such expensive armies when so many of their people were very poor. (However, the vast military spending of the rich countries of the world is just as offensive.)

Our first port of call in India was Amritsar. As we entered the city, it was the people who made the strongest impression on me. There were just so many of them. We had seen crowds in Pakistan too, but nothing like this. Cycling into Amritsar and other Indian cities was a bit like trying to ride through the crowds coming out of a big football match, except that these people were merely going about their normal daily business. They walked all over the roads, and we just had to pick our way through them. To begin with this was rather alarming, but our confidence increased as we got used to it and as the Indian people expressed their friendliness towards us.

We were very struck by the great contrasts of wealth and poverty which we saw in India — much greater than those we had seen in Pakistan. While many people lived in flimsy straw huts or tents and others even slept on the pavements, there were also quite a few rich people about. We saw sophisticated Indian ladies wearing costly silk saris, fancy hair-dos, make-up and jewellery, their conspicuous wealth standing out in stark contrast to the drab appearance of the impoverished masses. The reasons behind the width of the gulf between the rich and the poor are undoubtedly deeply rooted in the Hindu caste system, which legitimises a highly structured social hierarchy. However, there was also evidence of solid national wealth. India had a sound infrastructure with good roads and railways, many great industries and splendid public buildings and a well-developed if rather clumsy bureaucracy. In the towns, the buildings often seemed to be in better condition than comparable ones in Pakistan, and the side roads to the villages were also more likely to be tarred.

Although the rich had cars (usually Indian-made replicas of British models, since the country is striving towards self-sufficiency), the great mass of the people either walked or travelled by bicycle. In Pakistan most rickshaws were motorised, but in India most were of the good, old-fashioned, pedal-driven variety. So in a way we felt quite at home among all the human-powered bicycles and rickshaws, and it was an interesting experience to get caught up in a rickshaw traffic jam! We would be stuck in the centre of a town among thousands of cyclists and irate rickshaw wallahs, not a car to be seen, while a solitary policeman would try to control the pedal-powered mêlée.

While in Amritsar, we simply had to visit the Golden Temple, the world-famous Sikh holy of holies. A pedal rickshaw took us through the bumpy, congested streets of the city and finally brought us to a large, open area where numerous taxis and rickshaws were parked and where a great number of visitors were milling about. There before us was the Golden Temple, with one of its two longer walls facing us. This was not merely a wall, but was, in fact, an integral part of the Temple, and had many windows and doors in it. Beyond this wall, we could make out the domes and towers of the holy of holies at the centre of the complex. We made our way to a booth at the centre of the wall and there took off our shoes and socks and handed them over to an official who would look after them until we returned. After walking through a foot-bath, we then entered the Temple and came into its central quadrangle. The whole complex must have been roughly the size of a football stadium. It was open to the sky, and most of its area was taken up by a rectangular artificial lake. At the centre of this was an island, upon which had been built the holy of holies: a large, square, four-storeyed structure. It was topped by a large, centrally placed dome, four smaller domes at the corners and many others along the four sides. The entire upper portion of the building, including the domes, was coated in gold — hence the name of the Temple. A narrow causeway led out to the holy of holies from one of the two shorter sides of the lake, on my right. The floor of the great quadrangle was beautifully paved with black, white and peach tiles arranged in an intricate geometrical design.

It was a strange experience walking around the Temple among the pilgrims. From the holy of holies in the middle of the lake wafted the eerie sound of chanting, broadcast over loudspeakers, occasionally building up to an emotional crescendo. We felt rather uncomfortable and even scared, because these surroundings were so alien to us, but despite this, we walked out to the island. People were approaching it on one side of the causeway and leaving it on the other. We were too nervous to go inside the shrine, so we just moved slowly along with the stream of people circulating around the building and then went back down the causeway.

One rather amusing aspect of our visit was the rule which stipulated that people had to keep their heads covered while they were in the Temple precincts. This proved to be a slight problem for us, since the only head coverings we could muster were our two dirty handkerchiefs. No one seemed to be offended by this, but we did feel silly wearing them! And it proved to be no easy matter walking around wearing these flimsy bits of cloth, because if we moved too fast, they would get caught in the wind and would fall off! So we had to walk with poise, leaning slightly forward, being careful not to make any sudden movements.

Sikhism is a relatively new religion and came into existence during a period of religious revival in India during the fifteenth and sixteenth centuries, and is notable because its adherents discarded the traditional Hindu caste distinctions and adopted certain new customs. For example, Sikh men have full beards and grow their hair long, which explains the hair buns of the boys and the turbans of the men. Sikhs believe that the way of salvation is to regard God and not the self as the centre of life, and to strive to be devoted to God and to do good works. These are high and worthy ideals, and yet I found it sad that the adherents of this religion do not know Jesus Christ, the only one who can bring salvation, and that not by devotion and good works, but as a free and unmerited gift from a loving God.

From Amritsar, we set off through the Punjab, the most prosperous state in India. The roads and railways were now very good, and we noticed that there was quite a lot of industry around the towns. Most of the people were Sikhs, and they seemed very proud of their state. One Punjabi told us that 'every village has electricity and a paved road leading to it'.

But as we cycled through the countryside, my peace of mind was disturbed by the problem of the sprocket-block. It was only a matter of time before another of my spokes broke, so I urgently needed to get a new block. We had been told that the best place in which to try to get one was the capital, Delhi, but what if we couldn't get one there? We would have to stay put and wait for one to be flown out from home. That would be expensive and, because of the slowness of Indian bureaucracy, it might prove to be a very time-consuming business getting the block through customs. That would put us seriously behind schedule, and we would run into real problems if we didn't get out of Asia before the monsoons started. I prayed for guidance as to what to do about this, and was encouraged by the knowledge that many others at home were praying for us.

The problem was solved in the city of Ludhiana, where I managed to obtain a block of a kind which was manufactured there for export to the USA. Although it was not of the same type as my original block, it fitted perfectly. That was a load off my mind! I thanked God for once again getting us out of a tight situation.

As in Pakistan, while travelling in North India, we developed an entire chain of contacts, one set of people we had stayed with giving us the names and addresses of others further along on our journey. Since the Christians in North India were very few in number, they all seemed to know one another, and they were usually able to recommend to us people in the next city or district. Sometimes we would be given a covering letter with which to introduce ourselves to a new contact, sometimes we would just mention the name of the person we had stayed with previously.

As we moved in an easterly direction across India, heading towards Nepal, we often stayed at Christian mission hospitals, where we were always made welcome by the staff. They were used to visitors calling and had guest-rooms available for them. At Ludhiana we stayed at the Brown Memorial Mission Hospital, which we had heard about back home, since the Presbyterian Church in Ireland had recently helped to fund the building of some new wards there.

The administrator, Hanny Williams, a quiet, kindly man in his thirties, showed us around the place. I was a little concerned when he told me that private patients were admitted.

'Does that mean that poor people, who can't pay, aren't admitted for treatment?' I asked.

'Oh no, of course not,' replied Hanny. 'The private patients pay more than the cost of their treatment. The excess goes into the poor fund, which enables the poor people to get discounts of up to 100 per cent.'

I had been deeply struck by what I had seen of the plight of India's poor. 'Can't something be done about all this poverty?' I asked.

'Well, the best way to solve the problem is to introduce effective birth control,' answered Hanny. 'Some progress has been made in that direction, but one of the greatest causes of poverty in India is still the fact that too many children are born to the illiterate and uneducated. These people need education about birth control, but if a labourer takes a day off work to visit the family-planning clinic, he gets no pay and so his family have no food for that day. So the poor people are caught in a poverty trap: they can't afford to have so many children, and yet they can't afford to find out about birth control.'

During our journey across North India, we were able to meet and talk to people from many different walks of life. In Pakistan we had met many poor people and had sometimes stayed in their humble abodes and received their very generous hospitality, but in India we met a number of educated and influential people. John and I found it extremely stimulating to talk with them. At Amballa City in Haryana State we stayed at the Philadelphia Hospital, and we were treated like kings by the kind people we met there. I had a memorable conversation with a Dr Sukhnandan — a very thoughtful, serious man — about India and world issues.

'There is a real need for more Indian Christian doctors,' he said, 'since they are able to help the people towards spiritual as well as physical wholeness. We also need money from the rich countries of the world to support special projects like eye-treatment camps and community-health programmes.

'But, of course,' he continued, 'it is not only India which has social and economic problems. All over the world the wealth is unevenly distributed, and I think it is most iniquitous that rich countries are dumping grain in the sea in order to keep prices up, while poor people are starving.'

'I agree with you very much,' I said. It was such an encouragement for me to meet someone from a Third World country whose views on wealth and poverty were so similar to my own. 'I think the greatest disease of the rich West is materialism. People have become too concerned about owning lots of things. In a world where people are dying for lack of the basic necessities of life, people in the West are building great houses, driving around in luxurious cars and are enjoying every kind of luxury imaginable. It's a very selfish society, and doesn't take into account the poor of the world and the fact that our wealth may be making others poor; and it doesn't take God into account — a God who has shown in the Bible that he is concerned about the physical welfare of man as well as his spiritual welfare. What's more, this running around after material possessions doesn't even make the people in the West happy!'

'Yes, I do believe that possibly the happiest people in the world are the ordinary people in an Indian village,' said Dr Sukhnandan. 'They don't have anything except their fields, mud houses and buffalo, the men work hard all day on the land, the women work hard preparing food and looking after their families, and they fall into bed at night tired and sleep well until the morning.'

Hearing these things from an educated Indian man reinforced my own conviction that our materially rich and selfishly motivated Western society is an artificial and unnatural environment and that all our accumulation of material things does not satisfy the fundamental human yearning for something deeper, something real, to give direction and meaning to life. In India we saw many young people from the West who had gone there in search of that deeper meaning, who were disillusioned with all that Western culture has to offer — disillusioned with wealth, sex, drugs and all the other so-called excitements which our society provides, having found that these things did not bring them peace. And so they had come to India in hordes, searching for that peace; searching for God. What a tragedy that the Christian church in the West, which in the Person of Jesus Christ has the answer to the questioning and searching of these young people, has by and large failed to make him known to them.

In India, we stayed with Christians on many occasions, but we also had the chance to meet people of other religions. On 18th January, we rode into a town called Panipat, sixty-five miles from Delhi. After making enquiries, we found that there was nowhere in the town where we could spend the night. We felt edgy and nervous because there were angry crowds and baton-wielding police on the streets. Apparently there was going to be a nation-wide general strike the next day, and so there was a lot of tension in the air. We went back out to the edge of town to reassess the situation. Where were we going to spend the night?

Just then a man dressed in dark-grey trousers, a grey pullover and an orange turban and with his beard tied in a knot walked up to us. 'Hello,' he said. 'You are looking for somewhere to stay tonight?'

'Yes, we are,' I replied, 'but we can't afford to stay at the hotel — they asked us for 200 rupees!'

'That is far too much!' he exclaimed. 'But do not be

worrying — I know where you will stay tonight. Tomorrow the people will be striking. They will be very cross. But you can stay in a very safe place. It is the safest place in the town. Come with me.'

We were still feeling nervous after getting out of the tense crowds, but this man seemed kind and friendly, so we followed him. He led us along the road to a big gate in a wall. The gate was opened and after some negotiations, we were allowed through. It was then that we discovered that we had been admitted into the local Sikh temple. The temple itself was a square, blue building at the centre of a courtyard. Soon we were shown to a small bedroom facing on to the courtyard. We were then introduced to the priests and the holy men, all sporting long, grey beards and turbans.

The man who had brought us to the temple introduced himself as Jag Jeet Singh, and as he was the only one who could speak English and lived in a house across the road, we had to find out all we needed to know from him before he went home for the night.

'Is it possible to have a bath or shower here?' John enquired.

'Ah, yes. It is very much possible,' replied Jag Jeet. He led us to another door facing on to the courtyard. 'Here is the bathroom,' he said, opening the door. Inside was a small, bare room with two taps and a bucket.

'In your country you have customs,' he said. 'In India, too, we have customs. If you have bath at the Sikh temple, please be keeping your underwear on.'

Wishing to be courteous, we of course agreed to this, but not without a good deal of concealed amusement!

'Maybe swimming trunks could be construed as being underwear,' I suggested after Jag Jeet had gone. That seemed a good idea, and so it was that we managed to have a wash without going against the customs of our hosts — or getting our underwear wet.

The priests at the temple were very kind to us and their hospitality helped to allay the nervousness we felt about spending the night in the rather strange environment of a Sikh temple, which echoed incessantly to the sound of chanted prayers. That night they fed us very well with lots of rice, *chapatti*, lentils and tea.

In the morning, Jag Jeet and one of the priests took us into the temple. Its interior was simple, with a clean, tiled floor, an altar-like object at the centre and pictures on the walls. The priest gave us some rich, sugary sweets from the altar and then, according to Jag Jeet's translation, prayed that we would have a safe journey and would live to a great age.

Later that day, after some pleasant cycling on a new dual carriageway, we rode into Delhi, India's capital and one of the great cities of the world. My childhood dreams of travelling to distant, exotic places seemed to be coming true. What a sense of achievement I felt as we rode into Delhi, having travelled 4,000 miles to get there! All around us were great crowds, innumerable cycle-rickshaws, rushing black-and-yellow taxis and overloaded buses. With a feeling of elation, we passed from the old city into New Delhi, a very beautiful garden city with many fine, modern buildings, attractively arranged among tree-lined boulevards that radiated out from Connaught Place, the focal point of the capital. Delhi, with its affluence, fine public buildings, palatial houses and cosmopolitan atmosphere is the prestigious showpiece of India, and stands in stark contrast to the simpler, poorer character of the rest of the country.

As we arrived at Delhi, another of my back wheel's spokes broke. At the YMCA where we stayed, I got the new Indian sprocket-block off easily, using a wrench borrowed from a plumber. I was very fortunate indeed to have obtained a new block in Ludhiana since, as I later discovered, there were no suitable blocks for sale anywhere in Delhi. We would have been obliged to wait for one to be sent from home, with all the headaches that would have involved.

We picked up our latest batch of mail from home, which had been sent to the Delhi YMCA, and also collected the money which had been sent on to the State Bank of India for us. After getting our visas for Nepal, we went and saw the sights of India's capital, such as the teeming Chandi Chowk bazaar and the famous Red Fort, a bastion built out of red stone in the seventeenth century by Shah Jahan.

On our way out of Delhi, we stopped on the road beside the Indian Parliament building and asked a bystander if he would take our photo. He obligingly did this, but by the time the picture was taken there was a huge crowd of people on the pavement and the road, all of them fascinated by our bicycles. Even the buses and trucks had to stop, and we caused a big traffic jam. We quickly got on our way in case we were arrested by the police for causing a disturbance.

From Delhi we made our way to the city of Agra, which was about 100 miles south of the capital. Of course, while we were there, we couldn't miss the chance of visiting the Taj Mahal. It really was an amazing place, its white marble gleaming brightly in the early morning sun, standing out against the pure blue of the sky. Each of us went around the building and its gardens individually, while the other watched the bikes.

While at Agra, we stayed with Professor and Mrs Dass of St John's College, and enjoyed some more fascinating discussions with them and the students. However, it's an amusing incident at Agra which I remember most clearly. One evening we were dining with the Dass family and their friends, and the conversation was very stimulating. Mrs Dass had been watching me for a while, then smiled and said, much to my consternation, 'Eat nicely! Eat nicely!'

I suddenly felt acutely embarrassed. Wasn't I eating nicely? Was I committing some sort of social faux pas? But no, I couldn't think of anything I was doing that might offend my Indian hosts. So what had Mrs Dass meant? I glanced at John, who looked as puzzled as I was. I felt distinctly uncomfortable. Here was I, trying to appear educated and sophisticated, and I was apparently eating my food in an uncouth way! But then Mrs Dass smiled at me approvingly, and the pleasant conversation continued as before.

'What's going on?' I wondered. Mrs Dass' remark was completely out of keeping with the rest of her behaviour, as she had been most kind and hospitable to us. But eventually I came to the conclusion that I had misunderstood her. English was probably her third or fourth language, so sometimes she might not say quite what she meant. I guessed that what she was trying to tell me was something like, 'Please feel at home and enjoy yourself. Feel free to eat as much as you want.' Cross-cultural communication isn't always easy!

Continuing our eastward migration, we came to the city of Kanpur. On the day we reached it, we had for the first time cycled more than 100 miles in a single day. Usually we managed only about sixty miles per day at an average speed of twelve miles per hour. The next day we cycled over India's sacred river, the Ganges, and arrived at another big city, Lucknow.

At the city of Lucknow we stayed with the Principal of the Christian College, Dr Tewarson (an Indian national). He, his wife, John and I had some fascinating discussions on sociology and religion. Mrs Tewarson had studied the religions of the world and had noted that, as was the case with the other religions, much of

'Christianity' was in reality only man-made ritual and tradition.

'So having studied the world's religions, what would you say is the right way to God?' John asked.

'True religion — the only true way to God — is a living faith in Christ, a personal relationship with Jesus,' replied Mrs Tewarson, speaking from her own experience. And how I agreed with her, having myself become disillusioned with the ritual of 'churchianity' as opposed to real, living, vibrant faith in Jesus Christ. I found it so exciting to hear these things from someone not in Europe or North America, but from someone in India. What she had said reaffirmed my conviction that Jesus is not just for people from our Western culture, but for people from all cultures.

After Lucknow we headed north, approaching the mighty Himalayas with keen anticipation, though it would be some time yet before we could actually see the mountains. The roads were now very bad and the country was becoming increasingly wooded. At times it was almost like jungle. We even saw monkeys swinging about in the branches of the trees and dashing back and forth across the road. The people started to look different too: they had the slanted eyes typical of orientals, and their skin was a pale brown. This was what the people of Nepal would look like.

That country lay ahead of us now. It would be very different from the hustle and bustle of India. Nepal had only four proper roads, and large tracts of the territory were still inaccessible to the modern world. Within her borders were earth's highest mountains and extensive jungle peopled by isolated tribes. Nepal — so poor that it was sometimes described as the Fourth World, because Third World countries like India were rich compared to it; Nepal — also called the Roof of the World.

6

The Roof of the World

Ever since arriving in Asia, we had been cycling through great, flat plains, but now the scene was changing. In the twilight, I could begin to make out a series of peaks and valleys on the horizon, blocking our path from east to west as far as the eye could see.

'Just look at that!' exclaimed John. 'That must be the Himalayan foothills!'

We had crossed Nepal's border with India seven miles back, and were cycling the last ten miles to the little town of Butwal, where we would stay the night at a missionary guest-house. As we got closer, the beckoning hills became more distinct, and soon loomed high above us. But the terrain was still perfectly flat, even as far as Butwal itself.

The next morning, full of excited anticipation, we cycled over the last 200 yards of the flat, rice-growing border region known as the Terai, which was the last part of the great plains of the Indian subcontinent. Then, quite suddenly, the road began to rise and we had to drop down into first gear as we slowly powered our machines into the foothills of the highest mountains in the world. And so we started to climb thousands of feet, cycling along one of only two roads that connect the interior of Nepal with India, a road that twisted thousands of times as it followed one of the south-flowing rivers.

The condition of the road deteriorated rapidly and not only was it full of potholes, but often entire sections had disappeared in landslides caused by the monsoons. Often we found ourselves struggling through torrents of water or through thick mud or over areas of bare rock. So the pace was painfully slow, and during our first day in the hills we managed to cover only twenty-five miles. However, the slow pace also gave us the time to take in the magnificent scenery amid which we now found ourselves.

The valleys in between the hills were deep and green, with little wooden and brush houses dotted about along their length. The sides of the valleys were farmed in terraced fields. This was a clever system of agriculture which allowed the people to subsist in these difficult topographical conditions.

The people themselves were very friendly, and frequently smiled and waved at us. However, we could have virtually no conversation with them, since Nepal was never controlled by the British and therefore a tradition of teaching English in the schools never developed there. Of course, it's not every day that two Irishmen on bicycles ride through the Himalayan foothills, so our bikes and equipment aroused a lot of interest, especially with the children. They were usually dressed in rags and were barefooted, and would run along beside us for miles. They were such happy, smiling, innocent children, and it was so sad to think that forty per cent of Nepalese children die before they reach the age of five, because their malnourished little bodies are not strong enough to resist even common diseases that come their way. But this really was the Fourth World we were now in, and despite the country's wealth of natural beauty, the truth was that for these lovable children and their families, life consisted of a constant struggle for mere survival. In Nepal, we saw no evidence of wealth or the existence of a rich class, as we had done in India; here everyone seemed to be living in extreme poverty.

We still hadn't seen the snow-capped peaks of the Himalayas yet, not even by the time we arrived at the mountain-top city of Tensen. We stayed at the United Mission to Nepal guest-house there and enjoyed not only safe food and clean water, but also the cosmopolitan atmosphere created by the presence of missionary personnel from many parts of the world, some of whom joined us in the evening in a hard-fought game of Scrabble!

'When will we be able to see the Himalayas?' asked John after the game.

One of the missionary doctors, Dr Brewster (a Scot now living in Canada), knew these hills like the back of his hand. 'Provided the mountains are not shrouded in cloud,' he said, 'you can get one of the best panoramic views of them from here. I suggest you get up at six, when you'll be able to see them best in the bright early morning light.'

'In fact,' added Mrs Brewster, 'we could come with you and point out some of the peaks to you.'

That sounded a great idea. We didn't want to miss the chance of a lifetime, so we went to bed straight away.

In the morning, the four of us set out along the little beaten track that spiralled up the mountain on which the town was built. Below us were the terraced fields of a lush, green valley. But above the hills which surrounded us and much further away were the glistening white peaks of the world's highest mountains, stretching in a majestic, unbroken line right across the horizon.

'This is it,' I thought. 'I'm actually looking at the Himalayas. Heaven must look something like that!'

The silence and the stillness all around us added to the grandeur of the scene. Looking out on such a vista as this, there was nothing we could say; we could only stare in wonder. This was a time for contemplating the magnificence of God's world. The words of a familiar hymn of praise to God the Creator came to mind:

> O Lord my God! When I in awesome wonder
> Consider all the works thy hand hath made,
> I see the stars, I hear the mighty thunder,
> Thy power throughout the universe displayed;
>
> Then sings my soul, my Saviour God, to thee,
> How great thou art! How great thou art![1]

It was then time to get back on the road again. We were very happy about that, because it meant we would be getting closer all the time to those wonderful mountains and the views would become increasingly spectacular as we struggled north. However, during that day the mountains were out of view for long periods as the road meandered around the tortuous terrain of the foothills.

We were hoping to stay the night with Adam Kirk, an Australian engineer whose name and address we had obtained from the Christian expatriate grapevine in that part of the world. He lived with his family at a place called Andhi Khola and was working on a hydroelectric project which was supported in part by Tear Fund. After a hard day's cycling, during which we amazingly covered only thirty miles, we pulled up at a little wooden *bhattis* (tea-house) in a small town.

'Is this Andhi Khola?' I enquired of the people in the tea-house. 'Andhi Khola? Andhi Khola?'

One of the men pointed meaningfully at the ground in reply to my question. So this was indeed Andhi Khola. But where were the Kirk family? While John looked

---

[1] © Stuart K. Hine (transl.) 1953, administered worldwide (except USA and Continental America) by Thankyou Music Ltd, P.O. Box 75, Eastbourne BN23 6NW, England.

after the bikes, I went off to try to find out. After about thirty minutes, I discovered the Kirks' house and returned to John, who I found surrounded by inquisitive children. We then had to haul the bikes up the town's main 'street', which, composed of large, bare boulders on a very steep hill, actually bore a close resemblance to a cliff face. At one stage I thought we would have to use ropes, but the children, used to carrying great loads themselves, as are all the Nepalese, enthusiastically helped us scale the cliff face. Then, after negotiating a very narrow, precipitous path at the top, we made it to the Kirks' place, introduced ourselves, and were welcomed into their humble Nepalese mud-and-wood home.

Adam and his wife, Jenny, were in their early thirties and had four very lively sons aged one, three, five and seven. John and I kicked a ball about with them on the patch of ground at the rear of the house for a while, and then it was time for the evening meal of bread and soup.

'This must all be quite a change from life in Australia,' remarked John at the table.

Adam grinned. 'Yes, the house is a bit primitive,' he said. 'As you may have noticed, we don't have electricity or a cooker or even a kitchen sink. And yet this is one of the best houses in the area.'

'I see you keep your water in pots,' I said. 'Do you have to go far to get it?'

'Oh, it's not too inconvenient,' replied Adam. 'There's a spring a couple of hundred yards away. But many of the families here have much further than that to walk to get their water. Things are easier during the summer rains, though — then you can catch the water as it runs off the roof.'

'What sort of food is available locally?' asked John.

'Nepal is a Hindu country,' answered Jenny, 'so they have reverence for all life and don't eat much meat. So the food is mainly vegetarian — which is very healthy, as long as you can get a properly balanced diet. We're OK, because we get eggs from our hens and milk from our buffaloes. And since we have money, we can afford to buy important foods which are in short supply. But the ordinary people here don't have much money. One of the reasons why so many Nepalese children die is that they don't get a balanced diet, and so they're malnourished and susceptible to disease.'

'So how do you feel about your lifestyle here?' I asked. 'How does it compare with life back home?'

'Well, in many ways we have a much healthier life here than we would in Australia,' said Adam. 'The vegetarian diet is good for us, and our food has no artificial additives. And there's no pollution here — the air is pure and clean.'

'But life here is hard work too,' added Jenny, 'especially when you're looking after children. Everything takes a lot of time. I often spend literally all day fetching water, preparing food, cooking on the wood fire and washing clothes by hand.'

Our conversation went on for a while, but then it started to get dark. Since there was no electricity and the Kirks didn't want to use up their candles, it was then time for bed. John and I slept in our sleeping-bags on mats downstairs while the Kirks slept upstairs.

As I lay on the floor waiting for sleep, I reflected that my dreams of somehow living 'the simple life' were being shaken by the reality of Asia. I'd always liked the idea of living close to nature, without all the technology and sophistication we have in the West. I'd thought it must have been better in the old days when people ate wholesome, unadulterated food and had time for one another. But as I lay there hoping that the creepy-crawlies would stay away from me during the night and considering the very basic lifestyle which the Kirks had chosen to adopt, I wondered if there might after all be something to be said for the comforts and conveniences of the modern West!

Next day we set off on the last northward leg of our journey, before the immense Himalayan wall forced us eastwards. As we neared Pokhara, Nepal's second city, we were afforded tremendous views of the great Annapurnas (part of the Himalayan range). As we dropped down towards the town, the mountain known as Machhapuchhare or 'Fishtail' was a fine spectacle, glowing red in the light of the setting sun and rising many thousands of feet above us, proudly penetrating the soft, fluffy clouds which blanketed the darkening valley below.

Pokhara was a strange town, spread out thinly all over the fertile valley in which it lay. We weren't at all sure where the city centre was supposed to be. The place seemed in reality to be a collection of small shanty towns. There were no high-rise buildings and very little traffic. As we rode past the grassy field which was rather euphemistically called Pokhara International Airport, the city was thrown into darkness as the electricity supply failed. Apparently this often happened. Electricity was a scarce and unreliable commodity there, and often it would be diverted from one place so that another place could get its share of the power.

After spending some hours winding our way through the sprawling city, we arrived at its far western side, and after walking along a rough stone road for some distance, we arrived at Pokhara Boys' Boarding School, which was run by David and Anne McConkey from Ireland, two more contacts we had acquired from the Christian grapevine. We spent a very pleasant weekend with them, enjoying the family atmosphere of their home and some genuine Irish banter and cooking, the like of which we had not known since we left Rahim Yar

Khan in Pakistan. And, using our short-wave radio, we were able to sit in candle-light (there was no electricity at all that day!) and listen to the Irish rugby team defeating England in Dublin. This was truly a little piece of Ireland in the middle of Asia. I went to sleep with a comfortable, homely feeling, while the mountains of Nepal towered 8,500 feet above me.

On Sunday, John and I went down to the nearby lake, and there we saw many young people from the West who had come to Nepal in search of drugs, opium being a profuse plant in the foothills. Some were walking about looking shabby and dazed. Others were out on the lake in boats or were playing guitars and singing together. The Nepalese were making the most of it all by selling them drugs and just about anything they could at inflated prices. We didn't mind paying through the nose for our food, because we felt it was one small way of sharing our relative wealth with these impoverished people. We bought some succulent pineapples and some monster-sized bananas. In fact, they were so big that we could hardly get them into our mouths.

As we sat by the lake, a little Nepalese boy approached us.

'Please,' he said. 'Give money for buying book. Book so I learn English. I pass my English exam, but now I must buy more book — one text-book and one exercise-book. My family live on mountain and are very poor. Can you help me buy book and learn English good?'

We gave him ten Nepalese rupees, and as he seemed a bit hungry, we gave him a banana too. We wanted to give him more, but we had no way of knowing whether he was telling the truth or not. We felt it was degrading for him to have to ask us for help in this way, and we felt guilty because we had so much and he had so little. We had no choice about being born rich and he had no choice about being born poor, and yet we could see that we had a choice about how to respond to this situation. We had to choose between continuing to live unaffected by all the poverty we were seeing on our travels and deciding to try to do something to change the system which kept the Third World poor. We had a choice to make, but this Nepalese boy had no choices.

Our time in Pokhara was marred by the fact that due to an overcast sky, we could not see the Annapurnas, which were so near to us. In fact, the dull weather continued as we set off east on the two-day ride to Kathmandu, and it even rained. But the new Chinese-built road was excellent and we were able to make good speed down the valley of the Seti river. At Mugling the west-flowing Burhi Gandak joined the Seti, and together they turned south into a deep gorge which cut its way powerfully through the foothills. Thus the water that poured off the great mountains of Tibet made its way through Nepal to the plains of India, where it irrigated the land; then, after joining the sacred Ganges, it made its way through Bangladesh to the Bay of Bengal. We spent the night in a little wooden hotel at the confluence of these two great rivers. As I dozed off, I reflected that on our travels John and I would eventually reach the same destination as would these waters which were rushing past us.

In the morning, we continued our journey along the well-surfaced road as it hugged the side of the valley and rose thousands of feet. Eventually it left the valley and went through many miles of steep switchbacks which took us up a 5,000-foot-high ridge and brought us to the Kathmandu valley. Along the top of the ridge the road was made of very rough stones, and in order to preserve the circular shape of our wheels we had to walk for long periods. This allowed us more time to meet the people, especially the children, who would shout, 'Bye, bye!' to us long before we even got near them. Some of them proved to be budding petty entrepreneurs with a keen eye for business and would shout, 'Bye, bye, one rupee!' expecting to get a rupee just for taking the trouble to shout, 'Bye, bye!' Others were even more enterprising and shouted, 'Bye, bye, two rupees!' or even, 'Bye, bye, five rupees!' It was all good humoured and we joined in the fun, replying, 'Bye, bye!' dozens of times every hour. As we struggled up to the rim of the Kathmandu valley, I noticed some women and children sitting in a little terrace field, so I called out to them, 'Bye, bye, one rupee!' This was greeted with great peals of hearty laughter, and I felt pleased that someone from faraway Ireland had been able to communicate with and bring a little light relief to some beautiful people who, although sharing the same planet as me, lived in a different world.

We stayed in Kathmandu, the capital of Nepal, for three days at the United Mission to Nepal guest-house, where we enjoyed the company of the latest batch of missionaries to start their language courses there. We also had our first shower for a week! Normally we had a good wash every day on our travels, but it hadn't been possible for some time. The water at the guest-house was warmed by a solar heater up on the roof. We saw quite a few of these in Kathmandu, which due to its altitude enjoyed a good deal of strong sunshine.

The capital was built in a broad, flat valley and had few high-rise buildings. There were numerous Hindu temples, built in a pagoda-like style. Many of the houses were ornately fashioned in wood, with roofs of red tile or tin. There were a number of fine public buildings, such as the Parliament, the ruler's palace and the national stadium. There were also some good new hospitals.

While in Kathmandu, we had to obtain visas to enter Bangladesh, and as we hoped to cross to there from the eastern side of Nepal through the Darjeeling Corridor (a thin strip of Indian territory), we also needed to obtain a special permit from the Indian Embassy. This route would give us a longer and more informative journey through Bangladesh, because it would allow us to enter the country from the north rather than the east.

We both bought some souvenirs of this exotic and famous city, and I acquired for all of £6 a real Tibetan lamb and yak wool sweater to protect me from the next winter's Irish weather. Since I had recently finished reading Mark Twain's *Adventures of Huckleberry Finn,* I decided to post it back home for the grand price of twenty-five pence. However, the missionaries told us to make sure that the stamps were franked, or else they would be taken off and resold. They also told us there was a bakery in the city to which they had given a recipe for Western-style wheaten bread, so we stocked up with four very large loaves before our departure.

Kathmandu is famous as a terminus for the great overland expeditions from Europe. Over the years many thousands of people have ended their journeys at this oriental city near to the world's highest mountain, but for us Kathmandu was just a brief stopping-point; we had a long way to go yet on our trek around the world. So on Saturday 13th February we set off again, retracing our route for about twenty miles back over the rim of the Kathmandu Valley. Then we took the main road south, back up into the foothills. This road was very rough and steep, so for this reason and because of the weight of the week's worth of food we were carrying, our progress was very slow. We were heading for the mountain-top village of Daman, but even by dusk we still had twelve miles to go. Since we wanted to spend Sunday at Daman, we decided to press on and pray that wild animals and robbers would not bother us. So we put our lights on, gritted our teeth and slogged on and on through the darkness, finally arriving at our destination. It had been the toughest day on our trip so far, and during it we had climbed a total of 5,500 feet.

Daman was at an altitude of 7,500 feet, and when we arrived, the temperature had dropped to 32 degrees Fahrenheit, so we needed somewhere warm to spend the night. We were told there was a tourist lodge with an observation tower nearby, but we were too tired to bother with looking for it in the darkness. When we asked for an hotel, we were directed to a two-storey wooden tea-house or *bhattis*, outside which we parked our laden bikes. On entering, we came into a crowded, smoky room illuminated by a dim oil lamp. We sat down, exhausted, at one of the bare wooden tables, and a Nepalese young man came over and greeted us with a smile.

'*Namestey* [hello],' he said.

'*Namestey*,' we replied in unison.

'*Daal bhat*,' I said, meaning that we wanted some of this common Nepalese dish of lentils and rice. The young man nodded.

'What about ordering an omelette?' asked John. 'We could really do with some eggs after a ride like today's!'

'Good idea,' I agreed. 'But how do we ask for eggs in Nepalese?'

John turned to the man and said, 'Eggs?' and, 'Omelette?' but he didn't understand.

'Try sign language,' I suggested.

So John started acting like a hen, flapping his arms, clucking enthusiastically and finally producing an imaginary egg. Finally the penny dropped and the young man and several other locals who had been curiously watching these crazy antics burst into loud laughter. Soon we were tucking into a meal of eggs, lentils and rice — garnished, of course, with the obligatory hot chillies!

This was the first time we had stayed in a tea-house overnight. The owner allowed us to put our bikes in a little room at the side, in among the hens. Then we were led up the wooden steps at the gable end of the house and were guided through a room full of men, women and children, all sleeping on the floor in their clothes and blankets, snoring away blissfully. Since we were Westerners, we were given beds in a small room which we shared with two other men. And so we settled down to an uncomfortable night, sleeping unwashed in our clothes after a hard, sweaty day.

In the morning, I was awakened several times as people got up to leave. When there were no guests in the house but ourselves, we decided it was high time we got up too! As we stepped out of that dark, stuffy sleeping room into the bright sunshine, we were greeted by yet another incredible panorama of gleaming white peaks in the distance. Then we paid our bill and collected our bicycles, which were now, thanks to the hens, rather less clean than when we last saw them!

That day we made our way to the tourist lodge about which we had been told the night before. It was a small concrete tower with an observatory at the top. The man in the village who was responsible for the lodge opened the door at the base of the tower for us and took our payment. We then climbed up the spiral staircase inside to the observatory. This had large, steel-framed windows which afforded wonderful views on all sides. We spent hours looking through a telescope at the snowy peaks of the Himalayas. There was Everest, about 125 miles to the north-east. Once again I was enthralled by the amazing grandeur of God's creation and wondered how people could be so blind to the beauty of nature. I thought of the clear evidence of design found throughout the natural world in the complexity of each different organism, in the structure of each mountain.

In this peaceful haven at the top of the world I felt at one with my Maker, thankful that he cared about all his creation and that he had loving concern even for me.

There were beds and a gravity-fed water filter in the tower, so we were able to spend the night there. On Monday, after watching the sun rise in the east and the mountains changing colour from purple to red to pink and eventually to sparkling white, we left the tower and cycled the mile or so to the top of the pass at Sunbhanjyang which, at 8,199 feet, was the highest point on the trip so far. Then it was a long, slow descent all day as we dropped thousands of feet back down to the Terai again. As we lost altitude, the temperature rose and we began to experience the sort of heat we would be getting used to during the rest of our time in Asia. Down on the Terai, the temperature was a relatively hot, seventy degrees fahrenheit, while up in the cool, crisp air of the mountains it was only forty-three degrees. During the warm late afternoon, John and I came to the town of Hetuada and there debated whether or not we should try to press on a bit further. We knew that ahead of us lay the tiger- and leopard-infested jungle — that wasn't a place to be after dark! But there were still several hours before dusk, and we wanted to cover some more ground. However, after asking God for guidance, we felt we should stop where we were.

The next day, feeling a little apprehensive, we rode on south into the jungle and long before coming to the Indian border we turned east, along the east-west highway. The Nepal Tourist Board in Kathmandu had advised us not to travel along this jungle road, because of the wild animals and the lack of hotels. But we loved Nepal and wanted to make it last a little longer, so we decided to take this road, which would keep us in Nepal and would lead us to Darjeeling, rather than go back to

India so soon. Anyway, we would take great care in the jungle and start looking for somewhere to stay during the early afternoon, so as to be indoors well before dark. I hoped that during the day the occasional jeep or truck would be sufficient to scare any leopards or tigers away from the road. But when, after an hour or so on the road, no vehicle had passed us, I rang my bell to let any animal know there were humans around.

This east-west highway, built by Nepalese-Soviet co-operation, was narrow, well surfaced and ran over numerous wooden bridges. A ten-yard swath of jungle had been cleared on each side of the road, which ran straight for miles through the tall trees and dense undergrowth. It was a lonely journey at times, because we often travelled for long distances without seeing anyone at all. There were paths leading into the jungle and very occasionally we would see local people in ones or twos. But we were afraid to leave the road and meet them. This, after all, was a different world even from that of the foothills of Nepal, because this road had only recently been opened and few Westerners had as yet been this way. The jungle people were truly primitive, since civilisation as we know it had never penetrated here before the road had been built. However, despite the loneliness of the place, we were delighted by its wealth of flora and fauna.

As the day went on, we saw no sign of a town or of anywhere to stay the night, and we began to get anxious. Eventually we came to some clearings in the jungle and some houses built on wooden stilts, where some very poor families were trying to scratch a living from the shallow soil. Only after cycling seventy miles did we come to the first town. It was just as well that we hadn't pressed on for another few hours the previous night, because we would have ended up in the jungle with nowhere safe to stay during the dangerous hours of darkness.

The town of Lalbandi, located in a clearing in the jungle, was built entirely of wood. There was no electricity or piped water, nor any sign of banking or postal facilities. We stayed at a *bhattis* in a room measuring ten feet by six, into which we crammed two beds, two bikes and a little oil lamp. After that, there wasn't enough room to swing a cat! The roof was made of bamboo and the floor sloped very noticeably. Our stay cost us the princely sum of thirty-two pence. At least we were able to get a wash there at a hand pump. That evening we enjoyed a good meal of *daal bhat,* although we were a little taken aback when a goat galloped past our table and straight into the kitchen!

During the next two days, we cycled east across areas where the jungle was being cleared to make way for rice cultivation, staying the night in cheap hotels. The further east we travelled, the more the terrain and agriculture resembled those of India. Eventually we came to Nepal's eastern border, and although we wanted to stay longer because of the beauty of the country and the simplicity of its people and their life-style, we had to keep moving. We needed to get into the south of Asia before the heat there became unbearable, and we needed to be out of it before the monsoons started. Darjeeling and Bangladesh lay just ahead, and Nepal was now behind us. So we sadly said, 'Bye, bye,' for the last time to the warm, smiling but malnourished children and adults of Nepal and crossed the border back into India.

7
Bangladesh

'I just can't believe how hot it is,' sighed John as we sat under a tree, eating Nepalese peanut butter and *chapatti*. I glanced at the thermometer on my bike. 'Eighty degrees fahrenheit,' I said. 'That means this is the hottest day so far, by a long shot — but then, we didn't need a thermometer to tell us that, did we?' I mopped the sweat from my brow.

So we rested and sheltered from the oppressive heat in the shadow of the tree for an hour or so. Then it was time to move on, through mile upon mile of tea plantations, their bushes laid out in neat, evenly spaced rows. The road twisted and turned through many little mud-and-thatch villages, eventually leading us to the town of Siliguri, which lay just at the top of the narrow strip of Indian territory which separated Nepal from Bangladesh. As we rode into the town, there was no doubting the fact that we were back amid the hustle and bustle of India, because once more, there were those great crowds of people milling about in the streets, there were the noisy, dirty trucks and buses, competing with the goats and buffaloes for space on the roads.

We checked into a cheap hotel for the night, hoping to move on to Bangladesh the next day. But alas, during the night I had to make several very unpleasant trips to the toilet. Our old enemy diarrhoea was back again! In the morning I felt weak and drained, so we elected to stay put for another day, so that I could take some tablets and recover a little. While I settled into a new chapter of Dickens' *David Copperfield*, John went off to the local tourist office to find out about the train ride to the famous town of Darjeeling to the north and to ask how to enter Bangladesh. In Nepal, we had heard all sorts of strange stories about how difficult it was to enter the country from the north. According to our map, there were no roads at all.

Later John returned, but he didn't have good news. 'Well, I think we can forget about the trip to Darjeeling,' he announced. 'It takes the train ten hours to cover the forty-four miles to the town!'

That was a disappointment. It would have been great fun to have spent the next day, Sunday, travelling on that railway to Darjeeling, 7,000 feet up in the Himalayan foothills, and seeing the tea plantations and the majestic views of Mount Everest.

'And as for getting into Bangladesh,' continued John, 'we've got some problems there too. No one actually seems to know where the border is, let alone how to cross it!'

So we decided to stay at Siliguri on Sunday, and worry about crossing the Bangladeshi border when we came to it. I had another broken night's sleep, partly because of my bowels again, but also because of a certain Bengali mouse, which, having got into one of my panniers, seemed intent on eating all our biscuits and bread. I tried to get him out of the bag several times, but in the end gave up and let him get on with it. We could always buy more food!

Making some more enquiries on Monday, we found out that the best way to get into Bangladesh was by way of a place called Naldibari, so we set off for Jalpigeari, which was on the way. On Tuesday, after passing through many miles of flat, fertile paddy-fields dotted with tall coconut trees and tiny houses, we came to the border checkpoint at Naldibari. This was one of the few places in the region which was able to deal with international passports.

We had to wait for quite a while before the Indian immigration officer turned up at the checkpoint. This was evidently his first and very probably his last business of the day. He actually looked rather surprised to see us, or indeed anyone — but then this was, to put it mildly, not a busy border crossing. Since he had so much time to spare, he very kindly gave us tea and biscuits, and filled in all our forms with painstaking care. He also exchanged our Indian money for some Bangladeshi bhats.

When all the paper work was completed, I asked him, 'Which way to Bangladesh?' It wasn't at all obvious where the border was. There was no clue to its whereabouts in the surrounding countryside.

'This way,' said the official, pointing along a bumpy-looking road. I was puzzled by the complete absence of a Bangladeshi checkpoint in that direction.

'Is there a road to Saidpur in Bangladesh?' I enquired.

'Yes, yes. Very good road in Bangladesh. Bangladesh very good!' replied the official, smiling cheerfully.

I judged that that was about as helpful an answer as I was likely to get, so we forged ahead on the very uneven road in search of that elusive Bangladeshi checkpoint. But after cycling a whole mile, we still hadn't come to it, and the road had petered out. There were just paddy-fields in every direction. So we enquired of some villagers, 'Bangladeshi checkpoint?' They simply pointed straight ahead, so we had no choice but to struggle along the ditches which separated the fields for about an hour, during which time we must have crossed the international frontier, although it was anybody's guess where it actually lay. But even now, there was still no sign of the checkpoint. It was important that we got our passports stamped there, because if we didn't, we would run into big trouble when we tried to leave the country again.

Eventually we came to a rough dust track and followed it for several miles, asking directions whenever we could. The bridges along the track had been washed away by the rushing floodwaters created by the annual monsoonal rains, but fortunately this was now the dry season, so we were able to walk across the empty riverbeds. In the end, we reached a small settlement beside a railway line, which turned out to be the location of the border checkpoint. It was all of twelve miles from the Indian one!

The officials at Chilanati seemed amazed by the sudden surge in business they had seen in recent months. We were the eleventh and twelfth foreigners to go through the checkpoint that year! They were even more amazed by our mode of transport. They mentioned something about our needing a special permit for our bikes, but it was too much trouble for them, so they didn't pursue the matter. After all the red-tape was sorted out we were shown the road to Saidpur, which was in fact a very long, deep rut filled with dust. The occasional brick concealed in the dust made our journey a bumpy one. Sometimes there were forks in the road with no signposts, so we had to ask for directions, which were often contradictory. Many times we asked God to show us which way to go, and we also used a compass. Eventually, after twelve hours of dragging our bikes through dust and over stony surfaces, we rode into Saidpur on what happened to be one of the best surfaced roads I have ever cycled on.

As well as being one of the poorest countries in the world, Bangladesh is also one of the most densely populated, with an average of 1,300 people per square mile. Out in the countryside, we wondered where all these people were, but when we arrived at Saidpur, we decided that quite a lot of them were there! The brick-and-tin town was just jammed with people, and we felt a little alarmed at first. We wanted to get out of the crowds, but there seemed to be no place where there wasn't a crowd. Whenever we stopped, we were immediately surrounded by hundreds of curious people, none of whom could speak English. Once again, I prayed to God for help and guidance. Then I felt that I should go to the railway station. The people knew the word 'station' and directed us there. While John waited with the two bikes, I crossed over the tracks to the station buildings. There just happened to be a railway board meeting taking place, and several of the men there could speak English. One of them knew of a Mennonite missionary clinic, and arranged for a rickshaw to lead us there.

We spent the night there and in the morning were taken to another compound, where three Irish young women lived. Their names were Eileen, Nuala and Mary, and they worked for the Irish relief agency Concern, and after hearing our story, took us to see their self-help weaving and sewing workshops. These were long, warehouse-like buildings made of corrugated iron and bamboo lattice in which jute was prepared, dyed and spun. They were noisy places, but the people working there seemed to be happy enough.

'The women who work here receive wheat in return for their labour,' explained Mary. 'And their children are given two high-calorie, high-protein meals each day, and there's also a health department to look after them.'

So conditions for the people there were very good by Bangladeshi standards. But later Mary and Eileen took us to a place where things were not so good: a half-finished cinema building which served as a makeshift home for 200 families. All that each family had was a tiny piece of floor space, usually marked out with bricks in an attempt to create some semblance of privacy. Many lived downstairs in the dark, dirty main hall. The stench of urine down there was unbearable. Other families lived on the stairs, and yet more up on the flat roof of the building. This was the worst poverty we had yet seen in Asia.

Mary and Eileen explained to us that these people were Biharis, a minority ethnic group in Bangladesh. At the partition of the Indian subcontinent in 1947, many Muslim Biharis moved from India to the newly created Muslim East Pakistan. They were industrious people, and soon became successful traders there. But during East Pakistan's war of independence (after which she was renamed Bangladesh), the jealousy of the Bengali majority towards the prosperous Biharis rose to fever pitch and many of them were massacred. The Biharis were then reduced to the status of refugees, living in appalling conditions like those in the cinema we visited and awaiting the opportunity to move to Pakistan.

Later that day we cycled the twenty-five miles from Saidpur to Rangpur, where we met Jim and Mags Maguire from Shannon in Ireland. Jim was an engineer and had been working for Concern, but was now with the Lutheran World Federation, helping with road- and bridge-building projects. He and his wife made us very welcome in their comfortable home. In many ways it was a real relief to be able to step out of the Third World occasionally and enjoy some Western food and hospitality and also clean, fresh beds and even luxuries like stereo music. We had a very pleasant time together swopping stories of dear old Ireland and listening to Christy Moore and the folk group Planxty singing of the high, rocky slopes of the cliffs of Doneen. We also talked a good deal about the problems of Bangladesh.

'The people here are really desperate,' said Jim. 'Eighty per cent of the population are in a state of absolute poverty, eighty per cent of the children are malnourished and forty per cent of all deaths here are due to infant mortality.'

'Yes, some of the worst poverty that we've seen has been here in Bangladesh,' agreed John. 'What do you think can be done about it?'

'Sometimes we feel the situation here is almost hopeless,' said Mags. 'What can any of us do? We feel powerless. But we have to try to do something.'

'Aren't there some child-sponsorship schemes being run?' I asked.

'Yes, that's right,' replied Mags, 'and they're a good way of getting people in the West involved in giving more realistic amounts to the work here. It takes about £100 to care for one Bangladeshi child for a year.'

'But what really bothers me is the problem of communicating the terrible state of affairs here to the folks at home and getting them motivated,' said Jim. 'If more people in the West really understood what it's like here, I think they would be much more generous and radical in their giving. So boys, when you get back to Ireland, you'll have a very important job to do.'

And that was a job which we were determined to take very seriously indeed.

Amid the immense poverty of Bangladesh, we felt very grateful for the hospitality and good food which Jim and Mags lavished upon us. In the morning Mags treated us to a truly hearty Irish breakfast of bacon, tomato, eggs, toast and tea. And as if that weren't enough, she and Jim also gave us a number of extra provisions for our journey that only expatriate workers would be able to obtain in Bangladesh, such as Australian cheese, porridge oats and even soft toilet tissue! What's more, they even offered to take some of our belongings home with them when they returned to the Emerald Isle in May. So we were relieved to be able to hand over to them the souvenirs we had accumulated on our journey so far and to know that we wouldn't have to carry them the rest of the way. I left my Tibetan sweater behind, as there wouldn't be much need for it now, with the daytime temperature in the nineties during the coming months! We said goodbye to our new-found Irish friends, and looked forward to meeting them later in the year when, hopefully, we would fly into Shannon Airport from New York.

One of the things that struck me about Bangladesh was the amazing greenery of the countryside. Because the three great rivers, Ganges, Brahmaputra and Jamuna deposit their loads of top-soil in Bangladesh, the land is extremely fertile. Also, with so much water pouring through the country into the Bay of Bengal, irrigation is simple and inexpensive. In addition to these factors are the prevailing high temperatures and monsoonal rains. As a result, conditions for agriculture are ideal, and it is possible to raise three fast-growing crops every year. However, these advantages have in a sense been the country's undoing, since over the centuries the abundance of food has caused a great increase in the population, with the result that Bangladesh is now so overcrowded that even with its superb agricultural conditions, the country cannot grow enough food for all its people and has to import essential food-stuffs from abroad. Another factor in the country's population growth is Islam's disapproval of contraception and birth control. Children are seen as blessings from Allah, and so the more children a family has, the more blessed it is. So as a result, birth-control schemes which work in state-controlled, atheistic countries like China do not work in Islamic nations like Bangladesh. Moreover, the country could not afford to go against the teachings of Islam because of its very heavy reliance upon financial support from the rich, oil-producing Muslim states.

Bangladesh is very prone to natural disasters such as floods and cyclones, yet these disasters are not as serious as the ever-worsening human disaster of overpopulation. As we cycled through the flat, green countryside, we noticed that every available square inch of land was being cultivated. Even dried up seasonal river-beds were being used to grow rice. Yet even when there was such an urgent need for food and millions of people in the country were on the verge of starvation, it seemed there was still scope for human vanity and greed, because we also saw a good deal of land devoted to the growth of tobacco.

Since so many major rivers run through Bangladesh, the traveller is not able to get very far without crossing any of them. Some of them are miles wide. At a place called Nagarbari, the road we were travelling on to get to the capital, Dacca, ended on the west bank of the Jamuna. There we boarded a river ferry which, after a one-and-a-half-hour journey, left us on the east bank, some distance downstream. From there, we continued on our way through poor brush-and-mud villages, along bumpy, tarred roads towards the capital.

Cycling on roads in Bangladesh proved to be not only uncomfortable on account of the bumps, but also dangerous, because although there were few cars, there were many trucks and buses hurtling along the single-lane roads at suicidal speeds. It seemed that there was an unofficial highway code in operation which stipulated that the bigger the vehicle was, the more right it had to be on the road. So, if a smaller vehicle happened to be on the same piece of road at the same time, it had better get off! Of course, in this scheme of things cyclists came at the very bottom of the pecking order, so John and I had to get off the roads many times in order to stay alive. A problem would arise whenever a cart failed to get out of the way quickly enough in the face of an approaching bus or truck. We saw one buffalo lying dead on the road underneath a smashed cart — fortunately the driver appeared to have escaped unharmed. An even bigger problem would arise whenever two heavily laden trucks were travelling in opposite directions. As they rapidly drew closer together, the two drivers would try to out-nerve each other, waiting for the other man to crack first. Occasionally neither driver would chicken out, and the results were mutually fatal. We saw several pairs of wrecked, burned-out trucks by the roadsides.

The reason for this behaviour on the roads is to be found in the Bangladeshi outlook on life as a whole. With 100 million people living in a country smaller than the United Kingdom, all competing for limited resources, life is very cheap. No one worries too much if someone gets killed on the roads (apart from that person's loved ones). Anyway, existence for most Bangladeshi people is sheer misery, so they tend to have rather a light attitude to life. Why be too concerned about staying alive when living is so terribly difficult? Death is no stranger to these people, due to the natural disasters which periodically strike the country. It is a commonplace part of family life because of the very high infant-mortality rate, which is caused by malnourishment. In a booklet published by the Lutheran World Federation, we read the horrifying true story of a typical Bangladeshi family in which the wife gave birth to ten children in ten years, of which only three survived infancy.

So we had to exercise extreme caution when cycling. We had heard stories of injured people being left to die at the roadsides, such was the general complacency about death. Also, although we found that most

Bangladeshis displayed a remarkable acceptance of their lot and had a good sense of humour, we also discovered that sometimes they could be threatening in their behaviour on the roads. Sometimes bus or truck drivers would deliberately try to run us over or would pull alongside us and then squeeze us off the road. Once when a bus driver did this to us, the passengers seemed delighted and some of them jeered at us, shouting aggressively, 'Americano! Americano!' out of the windows.

This behaviour made us very conscious of the existence of a strong resentment among Bangladeshis towards rich Westerners and particularly towards Americans. Forcing us off the road was their way of getting a little of their own back and shaking an angry fist at the affluent nations which control the world economy to their own advantage. There is a growing global awareness among the people of Third World countries, and many of the Bangladeshi young people we spoke to believed that the poverty of their country was caused less by the gods or by fate than by the grasping greed of the West and by an unfair distribution of the world's resources.

Eventually, after dozens of hair-raising escapes from death or injury, we rode into Dacca at the end of February in a state of nervous exhaustion. However, the streets of the capital proved to be very different from the roads out in the countryside. In fact, riding into Dacca was like passing from the Third World into a city of a First World country. It is often said that no capital is truly representative of its country, and that was certainly true of Dacca, which with its wide, tree-lined streets and boulevards, its many grand, modern buildings and extensive areas of luxurious residential housing, stood in sharp contrast to the country as a whole, where the roads were bad and the mud-and-brush buildings were mean and grimy.

While in Dacca, we stayed with Steve and Grace Knox from Ireland, who were working for Tearcraft, the handicrafts arm of Tear Fund. They made us very welcome in their home and took us to see the HEED Handicrafts project, of which Steve was the Director. It had grown out of the HEED Programme in Bangladesh, which had been founded by a consortium of ten evangelical Christian relief and development agencies from various parts of the world, of which Tear Fund had been one. 'HEED' stood for 'Health, Education and Economic Development', and HEED Handicrafts was started in Dacca in 1977 in order to help fulfil the latter part of that name. Each year, 125 Bihari and Bengali people were trained in such skills as straw-art craft, carpet making, weaving, tapestry, dyeing and spinning. The organisation also ran similar centres in other parts of Bangladesh.

We had the chance to discuss the problems of Bangladesh with Steve and Grace while we were with them. 'Why do you think the people here are so poor?' I asked.

'Well, that's a very difficult question,' replied Steve, 'and the answer to it is complicated. There are a number of factors which have a major detrimental effect upon the well-being of the people — like corruption, for instance. It's an endemic problem here. You can hardly get anything done in this country unless you pay a bribe. If you refuse to, then things either move very slowly or not at all.'

'So do you mean that the officials often have the power to help their own people, but are unwilling to unless they get their pockets lined?'

'Yes, that's often the case,' answered Steve.

'We heard about that sort of thing going on in Pakistan too,' said John. 'Often money which had been earmarked for helping the poor people was eaten up by layer upon layer of bureaucracy, so that in the end there was hardly any money left to actually do anything with.'

'That's why organisations like Tear Fund are so important,' said Grace. 'Because they're honest and efficient they really get the money to where it's supposed to go, down to the grass-roots level.'

'Another big social evil here is the uneven distribution of wealth,' continued Steve. 'It's not just that Bangladesh is poor compared to some other countries in the world — even within Bangladesh there are the haves and the have-nots. For instance, there are 100,000 rickshaws in Dacca, and each one is operated by two men, one using it from the early morning to the early afternoon, the other using it from then until late in the evening. They don't own the rickshaws — they're too poor for that. All they can hope to do is scratch together enough money to keep themselves and their families from starvation. Most of the rickshaws are owned by rich operators who rent them out and reap big profits.

'And overpopulation is another major headache here. The people have large families partly because Islam forbids birth control, and partly because the more children you have, the more money they can earn for the family by working or begging. Besides which, because of the high infant-mortality rate, a family needs to have a lot of children just to ensure the survival of a few.'

'We've met some people on our travels who seem to be angry and resentful because we're rich and they're poor,' I said. 'Do you think it's wrong for a Christian to be rich?'

'I don't think there's anything inherently wrong with riches,' answered Steve. 'Wealth only becomes wrong when it becomes our god. I believe God blesses Christians with wealth not so that they can hold on to it, but so that they can pass it on to others. In other words,

Christians should be channels to enable God's blessings to flow into the world.'

While in Dacca, we also had time to travel around the city in a rickshaw. We saw the thoroughly modern New Dacca and also Old Dacca, a riverside city of dingy, narrow streets. While by the river, we tried to book places on the Rocket, a passenger boat which would take us by river to the town of Khulna to the south-west of the capital. We wanted to travel this way in order to avoid those lethal Bangladeshi country roads after we left Dacca. However, we were told that all the cabins were already booked up. We knew that corruption was rife in Bangladesh and that a little baksheesh can work wonders, but we were unwilling to give bribes. God seemed to honour that stand, as the next day we succeeded in getting two tickets.

So after a pleasant few days in Dacca, we rode down to the river and caught the Rocket by the skin of our teeth. It was not often that she sailed on time, but on this day she did. We dragged our bikes on to the top deck, having to struggle through crowds of people on the lower decks, and, having left our baggage in our cabin, locked our machines to the rails at the edge of the deck. Our journey from Dacca to the east coast of India had now begun, as our ship wound its way along Bangladesh's many rivers to Khulna.

The Rocket was about half the size of one of the ferries which sail the English Channel and was powered by diesel engines. Its name was misleading, since it chugged its way along the great rivers at a leisurely pace, and our journey lasted all of thirty hours. However, the boat's slowness gave us a perfect opportunity to take in all the thriving activity on the rivers, which are the country's main transport system. We saw many great merchant ships from all over the world, importing cargoes such as oil, coal, rice and manufactured goods and exporting jute products, tea, animal hides and skins, fish and paper. Then there were the alarmingly overcrowded river-buses, built of wood but powered by diesel engines, speedily ferrying their passengers to their destinations. But the majority of the craft were wooden sailing vessels, the design of which had probably altered very little for centuries. The rivers were crowded with these boats, and it was fascinating to pass among the motley armadas of overloaded craft, their tattered sails flapping in the gentle breeze, their thin crew members straining at the oars in the sweltering heat. All along the river-banks were the yards where new boats were being built. As we got further downstream, we passed through dense jungle dotted with very primitive villages. As we sat on the upper deck, sunning ourselves for long hours and watching the varied and fascinating panoramas slip past us, it was as if we were watching a film about Bangladeshi life, or dreaming the most vivid of dreams.

Towards the end of the day, great crowds of men started to ascend from the lower decks and gather on the upper deck. The faithful had come to pray — for Bangladesh, like Pakistan, is a Muslim country. The men unrolled their prayer-mats and, taking their bearings from the setting sun, turned towards Mecca. Then from many throats went up the cry: 'There is no god but Allah, and Muhammad is his prophet. Come to prayer!' And so the men began their devotions, repeatedly kneeling, standing, reciting prayers and then touching their prayer-mats with their foreheads. I was moved by the sincerity of these devoutly religious men.

However, I could not help but be privately amused when the boat took several sharp turns in its course, which unfortunately meant that the praying men were then no longer facing towards Mecca. With mounting annoyance, they repeatedly shifted their prayer-mats so as to be pointing the right way. When the prayers were over and the men filed back down to the lower decks, many of them cast dagger looks through the window of the bridge at the pilot of the boat, who had caused them such problems.

The next day we arrived at Khulna, and cycled along a well-surfaced road to Jessore, where we spent the night. The following day we continued travelling westward along the bumpy, narrow highway which is the main road in and out of Bangladesh. And so we left the country, and crossed back into India. Ahead of us lay a long haul down the east coast of that country, and immediately before us lay one of the most infamous cities in the world: Calcutta.

8

The East Coast of India

As we cycled along the main road to Calcutta, the volume of the traffic around us steadily increased. Soon we were passing grim-looking factories with smoking chimneys. Above us, jet planes which had taken off from Dum Dum International Airport climbed into the sky, leaving behind them a wake of pollution. A floodlit, tree-lined dual carriageway led from the airport to Calcutta, and here our first impressions were of a modern city. A great wall of housing blocks stretched right to the horizon.

But Airport Road was merely a showpiece, designed to impress visitors. The reality of Calcutta was very different. One of the immediately striking features of the city was the almost total confusion which prevailed on the streets. Everywhere trams, buses, taxis, bullock-drawn carts, rickshaws and bicycles struggled to get about amid a great, disorderly mêlée. Often the traffic lights were not working, and when they were, they were usually ignored.

Not only was there disorder on the roads, but on the pavements too. In many places these had been dug up when water or electricity supplies had been installed, but after this work had been done the pavements had been left unrepaired. So we had to pay constant attention to where we were walking, frequently having to step or jump over broken paving-stones, holes in the ground or heaps of rubbish. Also, the drains were often blocked, and so filthy water ran out on to the streets and over the pavements.

But the worst thing we saw in Calcutta was the people's quality of life. We had seen abject poverty in Bangladesh, but we were still shocked by what we saw now. In Calcutta, as in many other Indian cities, great numbers of people live literally on the streets. They work or beg there, eat there and urinate there. They sleep there, with the cold, hard pavement as their only mattress and the stars as their only roof. They raise their children there, and often watch them die in infancy. Words can scarcely express the sadness and horror I felt as I walked among these people, conscious that they were real human beings just like me: people with hopes, joys and fears; people who experienced pain, hunger and suffering every bit as keenly as I did.

However, although the poverty of its people is the most shocking aspect of Calcutta, these same people are the city's saving grace. We found that despite the harshness of their lives, they were optimistic and friendly and possessed a lively sense of humour. They showed an astonishing ability to accept their lot and make the most of life.

Another thing which struck me about Calcutta was the treatment of the animals. Hindus believe that everyone goes through an endlessly repeated process of life, death and rebirth. If someone has lived a good life, they will be reborn as a human being or may even escape from the cycle of reincarnation; if they have lived a bad life, they will be reborn into the body of an animal. So animals must be treated well, because their bodies are inhabited by human souls. This attitude contrasted favourably with what I had witnessed in Pakistan, where the people saw animals as little more than machines to be used for man's profit. However, it also had its drawbacks, since it meant that pests and vermin were tolerated rather than exterminated. I remember seeing dozens of rats running in and out of holes in an earthen mound in the city, and some of the passers-by were even leaving them scraps of bread.

While in Calcutta, we stayed at the Baptist Missionary Society guest-house, and collected the latest batch of letters from Ireland at the YMCA. We managed to phone home and assure our families that we were all right, and we also had a telephone interview with Walter Love, the presenter of a chat show on BBC Radio Northern Ireland, but the line was so bad that the recording wasn't good enough to broadcast!

We were glad to leave Calcutta, but the prospect of the journey ahead of us wasn't too appealing. We fully expected the 1,000-mile journey south to Madras to be gruelling and monotonous. However, this leg of our journey certainly didn't start off that way because, against all the advice we had received, we set off on the first day of the Hindu Colour Festival.

'Don't go out today!' we were warned by Mrs Koshe, the hostess of the guest-house. 'The Hindus go mad today! They'll cover you from head to foot in paint!' But that didn't bother me — in fact, it sounded like fun! So John and I got dressed in our worst clothes and set out on our bikes, bracing ourselves to face the flak. We managed to remain unscathed for quite a while, probably because no one quite had the nerve to throw paint at two clean and tidy Westerners. But eventually a roving team of paint bombers, emboldened by alcohol, took some pot-shots at us and scored direct hits, much to their delight. The barrage continued as we approached the bridge over the River Hooghly, west of Calcutta. Everywhere paint-filled balloons were being thrown, bursting colourfully on impact; buckets full of coloured water were being emptied upon the heads of passers-by from the top floors of houses; and yet more paint was being lobbed at pedestrians by people in passing trucks and buses.

The Colour Festival is a delightful custom, full of good humour and fun, and the paint is harmless and can be washed off. We tried to join in the spirit of it, becoming increasingly multicoloured as we went on our way. The people were at this mad, paint-slinging lark everywhere, even out in the countryside. In each village we passed through, we received a fresh coat of paint. In one village they splattered us with paint but then, concerned that we might be offended, stopped us and said, 'No harm! No harm!' We smiled to show that we understood, and then they tipped some more paint over us! I'm not entirely sure what the Festival was all about, but at least it gave the poor people of India the chance to have a little fun and to forget the harshness of their existence.

I noticed that conditions for the people were every bit as bad out in the countryside as they were in Calcutta. Many of the houses were not even made of packed mud, but were yet more crude, being made of thatch, leaves or even thick grass, and looked for all the world like unkempt haystacks. Again it struck me that the people who had to live in these vermin-infested shacks were just as real as me: like me, they laughed and cried, they got hungry and tired, they loved and needed to be loved. In those haystack houses lived bright, mischievous children, gurgling brown babies, thin, desperate, loving parents and sick and weak grandparents, dying painfully after a hard life of only fifty years or so.

As we passed through one village, we encountered a funeral procession. The thin, pale body of a child was being carried shoulder-high on a little bed, surrounded by mourning relatives. That child was one of the thousands of people who died of malnourishment in India that day. It is estimated that an average of 15,000 people there die of starvation every day of the year. The tragedy is all the greater when the deceased is a child: a little life that never had a chance, because the odds were stacked against it. But perhaps that child we saw was fortunate in a way, because if it had survived, its life would have been just a miserable struggle for the bare means of existence. The child would have grown up to be like the people we saw in the countryside: like the women who worked all day breaking up rocks at road construction sites — hammering away for hour after hour — just to earn a few rupees to keep their children from starvation; like the poor, ragged woman we saw crawling on her hands and knees on a dusty road, eagerly collecting the few grains of rice which had spilled out of the back of a truck. Passing through scenes such as these, I was appalled by the degradation suffered by millions of my fellow human beings who share this planet with me.

We were now heading southwards, and it began to get really hot. The temperature during the day usually rose to about ninety-five degrees Fahrenheit in the shade. We were cycling in the direct sunlight, where it would sometimes top the 100-degrees mark. That was quite a change from Ireland, where it rarely got much into the seventies!

So we had to adopt a new routine in order to avoid being out in the sun too much. We would get up each morning at 4.30, eat a breakfast of porridge, eggs, bread and fruit and would get on the road by 5.30, about half an hour before sunrise. When we set off, we had to have our lights on, as the roads would be crowded with buffalo-drawn carts and people setting off to work in the fields. The early hours of the day were relatively cool (the temperature not getting above the upper eighties), so we normally tried to cover our daily fifty or sixty miles before midday. Then we would check into an hotel for some food and water. During the afternoon siesta, John would read the copy of Leon Uris' *Trinity* which he had bought me for my birthday, while I would learn about Uriah Heep's latest acts of infamy in *David Copperfield*. Reading Dickens helped to make me feel that I hadn't completely lost touch with the English language and British culture amid this alien environment. At seven in the evening we would have a meal and would get to bed by eight.

Unfortunately this new routine meant that we had to keep unsocial hours, so it was no longer possible for us to stay at Christian hospitals and the like. Instead, we had to make do with cheap hotels and lodging-houses.

Fortunately there wasn't always blazing sunshine on the east coast. Several times it clouded over and rained so heavily that we had to take shelter for a time and then cycle with our capes on. To begin with the rain had the pleasant effect of cooling us down, and I had the very strange experience of shivering while the general temperature was ninety degrees. But later, when the sun burst through the clouds again, conditions became uncomfortably humid as the surface water turned into rising steam.

However, most of the time conditions were very hot and dry, and there was so much dust about that we needed to wash our clothes every day. So before going to bed each night, we would have a bucket bath ourselves and would then scrub our clothes, allowing them to dry while we slept. However, getting to sleep while the temperature was in the nineties was not easy. I discovered that by not drying myself after my wash and leaving the fan on at top speed, I could actually make myself feel quite cool and get to sleep quickly. However, if the electricity supply failed (as it frequently did) the fan would die and so the heat would keep me awake for a long time.

It goes without saying that in order to propel a 5½-stone bicycle between 50 and 100 miles a day, you need energy. So we had to eat plenty of food each day. Food was cheap, so we could always buy as much as we needed. But that wasn't the problem. What bothered us was the monotony of our diet. We could buy plenty of fruit, especially bananas, and whenever possible we stocked up with porridge oats. Occasionally we managed to get some eggs, but we could never keep them for long because of the heat. Sometimes we could get bread, but it was very poor quality stuff. The staple diet of the Indian people, and hence ours too, was rice. The locals usually ate it with *dhal* (lentils) and vegetables, and the rich might manage to have some chicken too. But since these foods were all so hotly spiced with peppers and chillies that we couldn't cope with them, we often had to eat just plain boiled rice on its own! Needless to say, with a diet as boring as that, we didn't much look forward to our meals. Often our food would be made slightly more interesting by the addition of some sour buffalo curd with a little white sugar.

On one particular day we had cycled from sunrise to sunset, right through the sweltering heat of the day, in order to try and meet up with George Smith, a friend from our church in Dungannon, at a city on our route called Vishakhapatnam. George was a member of the Gideons organisation and was attending a conference in Madras and seeing at first hand the Gideons' Bible distribution work in India. He had planned to fly to Vishakhapatnam from Madras in order to meet us. However, when we arrived in the city, exhausted after rushing to get there on time, he wasn't at the rendezvous point we had agreed with him. We waited for him for a while, and then rang the Madras telephone number he had given us. He explained apologetically that he had been unable to get a flight to Vishakhapatnam. Also, he had a bad case of 'Delhi belly' (diarrhoea) and so wanted to get home as soon as possible!

It wasn't George's fault that he had been unable to come, but we felt deeply disappointed. We had been greatly looking forward to seeing someone from our own church, and we wanted him to see us too, so that he could assure our families that we were keeping well and looking after ourselves.

And then, after a disappointment like that, we had to face yet another unappetising evening meal of boiled rice! In a way, I found this experience educational, since it gave me some idea of the depression, drudgery and dietary monotony which millions of Indian people have to put up with. However, I also decided there and then to do my utmost to liven up our evening meals a little. So the following afternoon, after we had finished our day's cycling and had booked into an hotel in a small town, I went out and started a determined search for a bottle of tomato ketchup! I visited one shop after another, but none of them stocked it. Whenever an educated-looking person came into a shop, I'd say, hoping they could speak English, 'Excuse me — do you know where I can get a bottle of tomato ketchup in this town?'

Usually the answer would be something like, 'You are wanting to get what?' or 'A bottle of what, please?' or 'Yes, yes — you can most certainly be buying a bottle of Coca-Cola in this shop.'

The shops never had any ketchup, but yes, yes, they could sell me shoe-laces or any length of cloth or any amount of rice. This wasn't exactly a life-or-death matter, but nevertheless I eventually asked God to help me find some ketchup in that town. I was about to throw in the towel when I noticed a little shop which seemed to sell luxury foods like porridge oats and biscuits to a richer-than-average clientele.

'Do you sell tomato ketchup?' I asked, expecting another disappointment.

'No, but we are selling tomato sauce,' replied the shopkeeper. 'A very good price — only twenty-five rupees to you. Top quality!'

The tomato sauce, in fact, turned out to be ketchup, and although I had to pay through the nose for it, it was worth every rupee. Now we could add a whole new dimension of delight and interest to our meal-times: one day, we could have just plain rice, and the next, we could have rice and ketchup!

The part of the world we were cycling through was not a healthy one, so it was not surprising that in the end both of us succumbed to illness. One of the major problems for us now was water. Cycling in such hot conditions, we had to drink large quantities of it — up to one and three-quarter gallons a day each. Unfortunately the water was always contaminated and carried a whole host of harmful bacteria, and so needed to be boiled in order to be made safe. But we couldn't possibly boil three and a half gallons of water a day; it would have cost the earth in fuel to do that, and we didn't have a container which was big enough to allow us to boil that much water. Besides which, if we had boiled the water, we would have wasted a lot of time waiting for it to cool down sufficiently so that we could put it into our plastic bottles. So in the end we had to use whatever the local people called drinking water, and use purification tablets. However, these were not completely effective, as we were to discover. And then, if drinking the water didn't make us ill, the dishes (washed in the same contaminated water) on which our food was served at the hotels would. And, of course, there was another major threat to our health posed by India's malaria-carrying mosquitoes.

One day, after completing our usual fifty-mile journey, we checked into a lodging-house at Rajahmundry in the state of Andhra Pradesh. After having my usual wash, I suddenly began to shiver and felt ill. I developed a headache, couldn't face food and felt very weak. I collapsed on to my bed and slept for two hours. When I awoke, the headache was by now a splitting one, my heart-beat was 120, my temperature was 104 degrees and I was sweating profusely. John ran off to try to find a Christian hospital and doctor, while I quietly thanked God that this illness had held off until we got to the lodging-house. If it had come on suddenly on the road, in the scorching heat and miles from any help, the situation could have been much more serious. At least we were in a big town and the chances of finding proper help were good.

John soon returned with a doctor from a nearby Lutheran hospital, who diagnosed malaria. We had been taking a prophylaxis called Daraprim, but it obviously didn't guarantee immunity to the disease. We also had the medicine for malaria with us, and I started taking it right away. But to make matters even worse, I also seemed to have contracted amoebic dysentery. There followed one of the most uncomfortable nights of my life as, delirious because of the malaria and in great discomfort because of the dysentery, I crawled many times to the toilet.

However, the next morning the fever ceased just as suddenly as it had started, and soon I was feeling well enough to go out into the bright sunshine to a nearby Chinese restaurant, where we enjoyed a good meal of chicken, chips, cashew nuts and curd. I spent four days recuperating from the malaria and dysentery, and then we set off again.

But only a few days later John also suddenly became ill. He felt dizzy and had severe stomach pains and diarrhoea. We were in a small town near the coast called Ongole, and there was no Christian hospital there. But there was an Indian clinic across the road, so we went there — but with some apprehension, because we had heard terrible stories about Indian health care. After the rather surly young doctor had examined John, he sent a scruffy young assistant to get something. He returned with some tablets and two small phials. The doctor then fished out a very blunt-looking needle from a dirty dish sitting on top of a gas-ring, and I realised with horror that he proposed to use the implement on John, who looked even more horrified than I felt. I had half a mind to tell John that he shouldn't have the injection, but I feared that his health might suffer more if he didn't have it than if he did. The doctor grabbed John's arm roughly and rammed the big needle in. John cried out in pain. Our horror increased still further when we realised that the doctor intended to give him a similar injection in the other arm.

This 'treatment' was followed by an hour of observation at the clinic, after which John still had his dysentery and also had two sore arms into the bargain. We continued on our way, but John was really no better. Despite taking Lomotil tablets in order to contain his diarrhoea, he still had to stop and disappear into the roadside bushes at frequent intervals. At the town of Nellore we decided that enough was enough; John had to get some proper medical attention. He took two more Lomotil tablets, and then we travelled by train down to Madras, where we booked into a nice clean lodging-house and John got treatment for his dysentery at a hospital. We decided that in order to be able to continue our trip around the world at all, we would have to give up any notion of cycling further south down the coast and on to Sri Lanka. We had had enough of India. It was time to get out, before our health was completely ruined.

I was deeply shocked by our experience of dysentery — not only because of the suffering it caused us personally, but also because by it we had shared in the suffering of the ordinary Indian people. Impure water is one of the greatest causes of disease among them, and great numbers of them die as a result of the diarrhoea and dehydration which accompany dysentery. We knew that the cure was to drink plenty of clean water and to dose ourselves up with glucose and salts, and we could afford proper health care in Madras. But most of the Indian people don't know how to deal with the problem and can't afford treatment. As a result, they die of this very commonplace illness.

We spent a week or so in Madras, resting, eating good food, building our strength up again and making arrangements for our flight to Singapore. Madras was a big, sprawling city with some fine old and new buildings, and many dilapidated ones too. It also had a very long and beautiful beach. There was the usual Indian poverty to be seen on the streets. There were great numbers of beggars, and we saw women collecting buffalo dung from the ground. This was then mixed with straw, flattened into discs, dried out in the sun and used as cooking fuel. I remember seeing in one of the poorest areas of the city a red tower topped by a hammer-and-sickle flag. This made me think of Christ's Great Commission to the church to bring the good news to all the earth. Where were the Christians among all this poverty? Yet the Communists were there, trying to improve the lot of the people. It was small wonder to me that several states and cities in India, like Calcutta and West Bengal, were run by Communist local governments. If Christians don't get in among India's poor and show God's love in word and deed, then there will be others who will try to win the hearts and minds of the people.

During our week in Madras we made preparations for continuing our journey. Our bikes were both in good shape, although John had experienced problems with his machine's sprocket-block similar to those which I had encountered with my bike. But after the experience we had gained in fixing mine, John's hadn't presented too much of a problem. The tyres on which I had left Dungannon had finally worn through now, after an amazing 6,500 miles. I replaced them with my two spares, which would hopefully take me all the way back home.

We had heard horror stories about the inefficiency of Indian bureaucracy, and at Madras Airport we experienced it for ourselves. Indian law demanded that our bikes should be treated as exports when we left the country, so we had to get them all wrapped up in paper and hessian sacking. Then our travel agent arranged to have them air-freighted to Singapore. But when we arrived at Madras Airport to catch our flight, we encountered a problem. The customs official examined our passports and asked, 'You have two bicycles for export?'

'Yes,' I replied. 'We have the documentation here.' I handed him the export certificate which the travel agent had given us.

He looked at it, but didn't seem satisfied. 'Where are the bicycles?' he demanded.

I assumed that he had simply misunderstood me, and I endeavoured to clarify what I had said. 'The bicycles are being air-freighted separately. The travel agent gave us this document to prove it.'

'No, no — this is not proof of export!' replied the official testily. 'You cannot travel on this plane.'

I couldn't believe what I was hearing, and felt my anger rising, but tried to stay calm and polite. 'But our travel agent had the bicycles cleared through customs several days ago. This is the form he gave us — look, it's been officially stamped by the customs people. They wouldn't have stamped it if it weren't all correct.'

'No, no, this is no good!' the man snapped back at me. 'You must provide proof of export. You cannot board the plane.'

I didn't know what else to say. What is one supposed to do when even the people in charge of customs don't seem to know their own rules? I turned to John in exasperation. He was just as flummoxed as I was. India had been so draining for both of us. The clumsy, self-contradictory bureaucracy, the appalling poverty, the disease and sickness, the impure food and water, the unreliable phones — we were tired of it all and simply wanted to get out of the country.

Just then another customs official came along and asked what the matter was. He was less touchy and officious than the other one and seemed to understand our predicament. He took our export forms, said 'One moment,' and went away. We prayed for all we were worth while he was gone. When he returned, he said, 'I have checked the cargo contents of your flight, and your bikes are on board. You are free to travel.'

Presumably the rules allowed us to air-freight our bikes without 'proof of export' as long as we were on the same flight as them. So we thanked the official and hurried off, thanking God under our breath for getting us out of yet another difficult situation.

As we boarded the Air Lanka jet which would take us to Singapore via Colombo, the capital of Sri Lanka, we felt deeply relieved to be getting out of India at last. Once we had taken off and I could see her coastline falling away below us, I really did feel like cheering. We had had a very hard time there, particularly during the past month spent struggling down the east coast. But then my thoughts turned to the people who lived in that country down there. I relived the walk I had taken through the streets of Madras the night before. No words could do justice to what I saw; no words could adequately describe the plight of the people who lived their lives on those streets — lives of crushing poverty and despair. On the filthy pavements the men, women and children slept, with the stagnant, flooded gutters and the noisy, dirty traffic mere inches away. Here a mother and child slept on a flattened cardboard box, using a doorstep as a pillow; there a solitary little girl slept naked beside a lamppost.

Yes, we had had a hard month on the east coast, but at least the hardship was only temporary for us. We didn't have to stay. For us, the nightmare was over. But for the people of India, it would last a whole lifetime.

9
Singapore and Malaysia

As we descended towards Colombo Airport, the beautiful island state of Sri Lanka lay below us. Unlike India, the country was very green and fertile, and there seemed to be many coconut plantations. The land was mostly low-lying, although in the centre of the island there was also a mountainous area, shrouded in cloud. At the airport we changed planes, and as we took off in the Tristar that would take us to Singapore, I felt sorry that we had been unable to spend any time in Sri Lanka, such was the appeal of the place.

Towards the end of our four-hour-long flight across the Indian Ocean, we saw the large Indonesian island of Sumatra looming up 30,000 feet below us. As Singapore Island came into view, we were told to fasten our seat-belts. As we neared it, it was obvious that it had a very different climate from that of India. The land was covered in thick, dark-green jungle and the sky was very cloudy. The city itself lay on the south side of the island. We passed over the great harbour, where hundreds of ships lay at anchor in its deep, blue water; then over the amazing array of tall, modern buildings which was the city's business district.

On our first approach, our landing had to be aborted, but we made it on the second attempt and touched down at the brand new Chungi International Airport, which lay near the city. This place was a welcome contrast to the drab austerity of Madras Airport. We stepped from the plane straight into a covered corridor and were conveyed by a moving walkway straight to the terminal's central hall. Everything seemed modern, spotless and sparkling. The immigration and customs formalities were completed in a mere thirty seconds, and we just gasped with delight at the efficiency and cleanliness of it all.

The very first thing we did was head straight for the McDonalds restaurant at the airport and treat ourselves to such gastronomic delights as Big Macs, French fries and strawberry milkshakes — delicacies our poor Irish stomachs had yearned for while they were being subjected to the monotony of the Indian diet. I felt so sorry for the people of India, but I was overjoyed to have got away from that subcontinent of heartache.

Singapore is an island of Western capitalism in South East Asia. Normally our culture's flashy materialism sickens me, but after the misery of India it was a real pleasure to be back among the bright lights, familiar brand-names and reliable products of the West. Everywhere flashing neon signs proclaimed the merits of this or that camera, hi-fi system or car. The people of Singapore seemed to be prosperous. Businessmen walked about in expensive-looking suits. Young men in blue jeans and T-shirts strolled in the streets with their beautiful, slim, black-haired girlfriends, who looked chic in their long, flowing dresses. I recalled the poverty-stricken people of Madras who slept on pavements beside open sewers, and found it hard to credit that I had seen such things on the same planet. Ours is a world of bizarre contrasts.

It was time now to find somewhere to stay, so I got out the list of names and addresses we had compiled on our travels and started going through them. Back in

Hyderabad in Pakistan, Stewart Enthwistle had told us about a New Zealand couple named Peter and Ruth Blackburn. We called them on the telephone, and got through immediately. What a joy it was for us to find that all the phones worked, after having to wait hours to make a call in India! The Blackburns told us that accommodation was very expensive in Singapore, but we would be welcome to stay in their spare room. It felt so good to be members of the worldwide Christian family and to be able to call upon our brothers and sisters for help and advice. So we took a taxi to their home, twenty miles away, and stayed with them. Initially the Blackburns said we were welcome to stay for a few days, but after they got to know us they said we could stay for as long as we needed to while we prepared to move north. In the end, we were in Singapore for eleven days. Peter and Ruth were very kind to us, and it was a joy to be in a friendly, homely atmosphere after the rigours of our journey through India.

Using the Blackburns' home as a base, we spent a few days seeing the sights, such as the famous Raffles Hotel, the Tanglin shopping centre and the impressive sky-scrapers of the business district. We wandered about among the quaint old back streets, full of pokey little bookshops and Chinese restaurants, and visited the big shopping centres, which sell almost literally everything under the sun, and usually at very attractive prices. Although the city had its historic areas, most of it seemed to be new. There were great, glass-walled business tower blocks and luxurious Oriental hotels in the city and big, elevated roads running across the harbour. Everything seemed modern, gleaming and clean, and there wasn't a piece of litter in sight. In fact, the penalty for dropping litter was a substantial fine. Another feature of Singapore which impressed us was the politeness of the people. In fact, the Department of

Culture had put up posters all over the place advocating the merits of courtesy and exhorting the people to smile and make liberal use of phrases such as 'Please', 'Thank you' and 'Pleasure'.

While in Singapore, we phoned home once again and had another telephone interview with Walter Love in Belfast. This time the line was much better and our phone conversation was clear enough to broadcast. The interview took place live on Good Friday, and we thanked all our supporters at home for their help and prayers, and wished them a happy and meaningful Easter. A recording of the interview was played in our home church on Easter Sunday morning.

People of Chinese ethnic origin formed the majority of Singapore's population, and there were also substantial minorities of Malayans and Indians. However, despite this, there was a definite Western ethos about the place. All the familiar brand-names such as Kelloggs, Heinz, Kerrygold and Kentucky Fried Chicken were to be found. I had never dreamed that I would ever get really excited about eating a Weetabix, but I did in Singapore. It was delicious with sugar, bananas and milk, and eating it felt just like coming home. I got equally excited about eating Western-style bread and strawberry jam. Another thing I really appreciated was being able to drink water straight out of a tap, for the first time since leaving Austria. We didn't have to boil it or use purification tablets! In India we had been deprived of many of the little things in life which we had always taken for granted, and there was an intense pleasure in being able to enjoy them again now.

Most of the ethnic Chinese people we met impressed us very much with their politeness, friendliness and hospitality. In that respect, they could teach some of us Christians a thing or two. However, one aspect of life in Singapore we didn't like was the people's intense preoccupation with money. On one occasion, John and I got trapped for an hour and a half by a salesman in a camera shop who simply wouldn't give up trying to sell me a lens which I didn't even want. I'd never before encountered such a hard sell! I thought it was sad that people should expend so much time and energy on making money, when there are more important things in life. The same criticism could, of course, be made of a great many people in the West, who live in the same cut-throat capitalist system as the people of Singapore. So although it was a relief for us to be amid the familiar Westernness of Singapore after the misery of India, we could still appreciate that the poorer countries of the world had some things to teach the richer ones.

All good things have to come to an end, and eventually it was time to think about moving on again. We went to the airport to get our bikes taken out of storage, but were dismayed to find that the wheels of my machine had been crushed by something heavy during transit! However, fortunately we were able to get two new rims fitted at a repair shop in Singapore. I thanked God that this hadn't happened at Karachi, as it would have been impossible to replace the rims there.

On Friday 17th April, we said goodbye to the Blackburns and set off on our long journey northwards. We cycled through Singapore City — along its wide, modern roads, past the big housing blocks of the suburbs and the tall skyscrapers of the city centre. Then we headed across the island. Here the road was just as good, although the surroundings changed. Thick jungle was all around us, and the road was dotted with little shops and garages. Often these were old-fashioned wooden buildings with tin roofs; we seemed to have left behind the shining modernity of the big city.

We came to the long, busy, stone-built causeway which linked the island of Singapore to the mainland. Ahead of us lay the peninsula of Malaya, which was part of the state of Malaysia. (The other half of this country lay on the far side of the South China Sea, on the island of Borneo.) We crossed the causeway, with the open sea on either side of us. At the end of it was the coastal town of Johor Baharu. Like the rest of Malaya, it had its modern buildings and apparently a thriving economy, but it wasn't in the same league as Singapore. It wasn't as clean, but then, compared to the Indian subcontinent, it was spotless! Since they were both really part of the same landmass, Malaya, of course, had a similar climate to Singapore. They were just a few degrees north of the Equator, so they were hot and humid. But surprisingly they were not as hot as India, and the temperature usually stayed around ninety degrees. Also, unlike India, they had a lot of cloud cover, so it was possible to be out of the direct sun for long periods. However, the presnce of all that cloud cover also meant that there was a lot of rain. And when it rains in South East Asia, it really does rain! In fact, we were unable to leave Johor on the Saturday because of torrential downpours. Repeatedly the heavens opened for an hour or two at a time. We got caught out in the open by one of the cloudbursts and took shelter in a nearby hut. Within half an hour, the road beside us had become a river, and the five-foot-deep gullies at the roadside were soon brimming over. The passing buses and cars were crawling along at a snail's pace, their windscreen wipers furiously trying to swish away the deluge. After waiting around for an hour, we got fed up and decided to make a dash for the bus shelter on the other side of the road. It took us just a few seconds to cross the ten yards to the shelter, but that was enough time for the rain to soak us through to the skin. After what seemed like several years, the rain at last stopped and the sun came out, and turned the water on the ground into great clouds of sticky, humid steam.

Obviously, a country with such a wet, hot climate is ideal for agriculture, and this is one of the reasons why Malaysia's economy has grown so rapidly since she gained independence from Britain in 1957. As we cycled north up the peninsula, we noticed that large areas of jungle had been cleared to make way for rubber-tree plantations and crops like coconuts, fruit and rice.

Strangely enough, even though we had always managed to avoid sunburn while in the scorching heat of India, it now became a problem for us, because we were much nearer to the Equator and the sun was virtually overhead for several hours a day. This meant that our arms and upper legs were exposed to the sun's vertically descending rays for long periods, so we had to use a lot of protection cream and also cover up our limbs. That was very uncomfortable in these humid conditions.

Since there was really no cool period of the day here and it would be hot and sticky whenever we chose to cycle, we abandoned the early morning cycling routine we had used in India and kept more sociable hours, which happily meant that we would be able to meet people on our travels once again. There were many enthusiastic Christians in Malaya, as there had been in Singapore, and we looked forward to meeting some of them. During that weekend at Johor, we found a Chinese church where the people could speak English. There was a very happy and lively atmosphere in the service, and many young people were present. The assistant minister there gave us a list of all the churches and pastors in the country, so that we would be able to find help wherever we were.

So we set off on the main road which ran north up the peninsula of Malaya, all the way to Bangkok, the capital of Thailand. For much of the way, it was a very busy, well-surfaced dual carriageway, so, not wishing to share our journey through Malaya with fast buses, big trucks and endless streams of cars, we turned off the main road at a place called Yong Peng and headed towards the west coast.

Our first port of call on the coast was Malacca, which had at one time been a Portuguese colony, and then a Dutch one. The town was a mixture of smart, new concrete-and-glass commercial buildings and old edifices from the colonial period. I was particularly struck by Christ Church, built in the eighteenth century in typically Dutch style with pink bricks specially imported from Holland! We stayed at a guest-house run by a local Chinese Methodist church, and met the assistant minister, Mr Gan Mang Tee. He told us a great deal about life in Malaysia, including its politics, its culture, its wildlife and even its cuisine. In fact, for me Chinese cooking is one of the greatest delights in life, and in Malaya there was plenty of it to be had, since because of the presence of a large Chinese community, Chinese restaurants abounded, offering every delicacy conceivable. In addition to the restaurants, there were hawkers on tricycles who could cook up a delicious meal for one there and then. A typical instant menu would be soup, lightly cooked vegetables and shoots, nuts and meat, noodles and rice and fresh guavas, oranges and pineapples. The hawkers also sold all kinds of cold drinks. Our favourite was sugar-cane syrup with iced water. This was very refreshing in such a hot, humid climate.

While we were staying at the guest-house, Mrs Wang, the warden, cooked us some delicious Chinese meals, but Gan insisted that we should try to use chop-sticks! The Chinese onlookers laughed wildly at the weird manual contortions John and I got ourselves into. Using two chop-sticks in one hand was no easy matter, and, despite our best attempts, nothing was getting into our mouths. Those elusive noodles just didn't seem to want to co-operate. Our heads got progressively nearer to our bowls, but that didn't help. I tried holding one chop-stick in each hand, but even that was no use. After some patient instruction from Gan and Mrs Wang, I actually managed to get one end of a strand of noodle into my mouth and, fearful that I would lose it, I sucked up the rest into my mouth. That wasn't the right way to do it, and the noodle slapped messily on my face, but at least it was a start. Meanwhile, John had also been making some progress and had succeeded in getting a meat-ball nicely suspended between his chop-sticks. But then disaster struck: he dropped it from mouth height and it landed in his soup with a great splash! During our time in the Orient, we had plenty more practice with these eating utensils, and eventually learned how to use them properly.

Ever conscious that we needed to be out of South East Asia before the monsoon rains started in two months' time, we pressed steadily northwards, keeping to the side roads that ran along the coast. The scenery was truly beautiful. On our left, the luxuriant greenery of the forest extended right up to the edge of the beaches, where we often saw people lying in the shade of the coconut trees which leaned out over the hot, beige-coloured sand. Pulled up on the shore and moored out on the clear, blue water were rubber dinghies and little boats with brightly coloured sails. Occasionally we would see small islands on the western horizon, and in the east were the distant green hills of the central highlands.

As we passed through the towns and villages, we had the chance to get a first-hand look at Malaysian rural life. We saw the workers in the rubber plantations, bleeding the trees and collecting the precious sap in bowls; the women, wearing cone-shaped hats to protect their heads from the sun, stooping down in the rice fields, planting next year's crop; the teams of oxen pulling ploughs across the flooded ground. The people usually had simple clothes — the men wore shirts and shorts and the women shirts and calf-length skirts — but they looked fairly prosperous. Their houses were made of wood and corrugated iron and usually had electricity. Many of them were built on stilts, since, because there was so much rainfall, there were frequent floods. Many families seemed to own a television set and a Japanese car, although outside some of the little homesteads were old-fashioned carts with enormous, five-foot-diameter wheels. In the towns people were more smartly dressed and the houses were built of more durable materials.

On the whole the roads were good, although when we came to the River Linggi, we found that there was no bridge; the road just stopped at the river-bank.

'This is crazy!' I said. 'How do people get to the other side?'

'There's someone over by the bank with a boat,' said John. 'Let's see if he'll take us across.'

So using sign language, we negotiated a price with the boatman and cautiously loaded our heavy bikes on to his small craft. We were then speedily whisked over to the far bank. Getting the bikes out of the boat again was a tricky business, as we could easily have ended up in the river, but we got up on to the bank without any mishap.

Much of the time we were cycling through dense jungle, and, needless to say, sometimes encountered some exotic wildlife. On one occasion, I saw something moving on the side of the road up ahead of me. I applied my brakes, wondering what it could be. It turned out to be the largest lizard I had ever seen. It was all of four feet long, had short, fat legs, a squat, brown body and a long, strong tail. I really don't like reptiles much, so I was a bit scared. I don't mind them if they're safely locked up behind bars in a zoo where they can't get at you, but I didn't enjoy meeting such a big one out in the open. However, the feeling seemed to be mutual, and the lizard quickly scampered off back into the undergrowth. I couldn't blame him for being frightened. It's not every day that a bearded Irishman cycles through the jungles of Malaysia!

Some distance north of Malacca, we stopped off on the seashore and went for a very pleasant, cool swim. However, we had heard about the poisonous sea-snakes which lived in these waters, so we didn't stay in too long! In the evening, we sat on the beach beneath the coconut trees and watched the local people fishing for prawns by lamplight.

At a coastal town called Port Dickson we stayed in our first Asian youth hostel, after which we went inland to Seremban, where we stayed with a Chinese Baptist pastor named Mr Tan. He wrote out some letters of introduction in Chinese for us, so that we would be able to stay with other Christians on our journey through Malaysia. We spent a very pleasant evening of conversation with him and his family, and discovered that Mrs Tan was a gifted musician who had conducted a Singaporean choir which had won an international singing competition in Wales. Pastor Tan had lived in Hong Kong for some years and told us a fascinating though macabre story about the eating habits of the wealthy classes there. Apparently some of them got together once a year for a week-long banquet consisting of 100 courses! In one of the highlights of this gastronomic extravaganza, a live monkey was suspended in a hole in the table, with its head protruding above the surface. One of the diners would then take up a meat cleaver, cut open the animal's head, add some spices to the contents, stir them up and serve the delicacy to those at the table!

We spent the weekend at Kuala Lumpur, the capital of Malaysia, where we stayed with Peter and Sue Wong, whose names we had been given by a Chinese Christian in Singapore. Peter was the pastor of a church and on the Sunday morning I was given the opportunity to speak (through an interpreter) to the congregation about what John and I were doing and the reasons behind it. Even though I made it very clear that money for the Tear Fund Sob Tuang Refugee Camp in Thailand was being raised only in Northern Ireland, the elders of the church still got together and presented us with 100 Malaysian dollars (about £25). John and I were very touched by their spontaneous generosity.

Peter and Sue took us for a drive around the capital. The city was growing rapidly and had a good road system and many attractive modern buildings, such as the national mosque, which had a very unusual folded roof resembling a half-closed umbrella. The streets were ablaze with neon signs advertising a plethora of Japanese consumer goods, and the city's young people were stylish and flamboyant, although some of the older generation seemed a little poorer than them. Many people were eating out at restaurants at tables on the pavements, while the cooks prepared their meals in woks. Peter and Sue told me that the churches in the city were very alive and enthusiastic, although the majority of the population were Muslim.

After Kuala Lumpur, we got on the road that would take us inland over the central highlands via Bentong and Bukit Fraser (Fraser's Hill in English) and then back down to the western seaboard again. On this leg of our journey, we often stayed with Christian contacts we had made earlier or slept in cheap hotels.

The terrain through which we were passing was thickly forested and teeming with wildlife. Everywhere there were multicoloured birds and countless exotic butterflies. It was in this jungle region that I came face to face with one of the most dangerous creatures living on the face of the earth. I was cycling along the quiet road at a fairly brisk pace when I felt the wheels run over a bump. Wondering what it was, I stopped and looked round. I was horrified to discover that I had just run over a black cobra, said to be the only snake which will attack man without provocation. It can't have been too pleased about me cycling over it, as it was hissing and biting at the air in my direction. I wondered whether I had seriously injured it. Should I go back and put it out of its misery with a sound crack over the head with my cycle pump? But then, the snake would be just as likely to succeed in putting me out of my misery! It coiled away into the undergrowth beside the road, and I felt no inclination to go after it.

On Saturday 1st May we cycled into Butterworth, a town on the east coast, and took a ferry to Penang Island, known as the Pearl of the Orient because of its great beauty. It certainly was one of the most delightful places I've ever visited, with glorious beaches and a wonderful tropical climate.

We wanted to stop off there because Maureen Hider at Rahim Yar Khan had given us the name of Yim Fong Chung, who had studied with her at London Bible College and whose family lived on the Island. We called at the Chungs' house, but found that Yim Fong was working down in Kuala Lumpur at the time. But her sister, Yim Chan, arranged for us to stay at a Christian guest-house. The Chung family made us very welcome, and we spent quite a lot of time with Yim Chan, who showed us the sights of Georgetown, the Island's capital.

There were many fascinating things to see, such as a temple housing the third largest reclining Buddha statue in the world, and the Pagoda of Ten Thousand Buddhas, which contained great numbers of statues of the religious leader. This was the first time we had come across Buddhism in our travels. About half the people of Malaysia were Muslims, and about a quarter were Buddhists and adherents to Chinese religions, while the remainder were either Christians, Hindus or animists. From now on, we would see Buddhist temples with increasing regularity, since the border with Thailand, the only officially Buddhist country we would pass through on our journey, was just a day's cycling away. In Thailand was the Tear Fund refugee camp, the needs of which we hoped to publicise through our trip around the world, so we were very eager to visit it.

On the Sunday morning Yim Chan took us to her church, the Penang Full Gospel Church. The service was very lively and was followed by a celebration of the Lord's Supper. Afterwards, Yim Chan asked us, 'Did you enjoy the service?'

'Yes, very much,' answered John. 'It's always good to meet and worship with other Christians.'

'We find there's an amazing bond between us,' I said, 'even though we come from different countries and cultures.'

'That's right,' agreed Yim Chan. 'We are all one in Christ Jesus. I'm so glad that I'm a Christian now.'

'What were you before you became a Christian?' asked John.

'I was brought up as a Buddhist, as all our family were. But now my sister, my two brothers and I are all Christians, and only our parents hold to the old religion. We are praying for them.'

'I'd noticed some little Buddhist images in your home,' I remarked, 'so I'd guessed your parents weren't Christians.'

'I pray that my parents will turn to Christ,' said Yim Chan. 'There is so much superstition in Buddhism. I'm so glad to be free from all of that, and I wish that they were too.'

In the afternoon, Yim's father treated us all to a meal at a restaurant by the seashore. On the menu were pork, squid, oysters, chicken, fish, vegetables, bamboo shoots, crisps, salad, mushrooms and liver. Fortunately John and I missed none of this, as we were now fairly adept in the use of chop-sticks!

There was a lot of lively conversation during the meal, and towards the end Mr Chung asked John and I about our journey.

'So you are going to Thailand next?' he asked.

'Yes,' John replied, 'we hope to spend the next two or three weeks there.'

'They're going to cycle all the way up to Bangkok, and then they're going north to a refugee camp on the border with Laos,' explained Yim Chan.

'We've heard stories that it's dangerous in Thailand,' I said. 'Do you know anything about that?' I asked Mr Chung.

'My work takes me to Thailand quite a lot,' he replied. 'I go there by car, but I don't think I would like to go by bicycle!'

'Why not?' asked John.

'Well, there are more poor people there than here, and there is no shortage of guns, so it must be tempting for them to rob people. Also, Laos and Cambodia are unstable neighbours, so perhaps their troubles spill over into Thailand.'

'So do you think it's safe for us to go there?' I asked.

'Er ... I don't know ... I don't know ...'

Mr Chung's uncertainty did nothing to allay our fears! We knew that Thailand, although called the Land of Smiles because of the sunny disposition of its people, was also probably the most dangerous country we would pass through on our way around the world. In Malaysia we had heard frightening reports of the high incidence of robbery and murder there. Thailand was a very violent place and even the Thai Tourist Board in Singapore had issued us with a booklet entitled *Do and Don't in Thailand.* So as we said goodbye to the Chungs on the Monday morning and left the safety of Penang, setting off north once more, I felt distinctly uneasy for the first time on the trip. We had been in a number of tricky situations so far, but never before had I felt as afraid as I was now. Was this anxiety merely the result of what I had heard about Thailand, or was it some kind of premonition?

10
The Land of Smiles

Having passed through the Malaysian customs post, we started out on the last half mile to the border, which lay at the top of a gentle hill. As we cycled along the straight road, dense jungle on either side of us, it was hot, humid and very quiet. Only the singing and squawking of birds broke the silence.

As we neared the top of the hill, we passed a Malaysian flag, hanging lifeless on a pole. And then a Malaysian army camp came into view, crowded with soldiers and military vehicles and equipment. The exact location of the border was marked by a red-and-white wooden barrier across the road and by a high, barbed-wire fence which stretched to the left and the right through the jungle as far as the eye could see. It was guarded by sentry towers, one of which stood at the border crossing. A rough military road ran along the Malaysian side of the fence, and there were great rolls of barbed wire lying about everywhere. At the time I wondered what the reason behind all this military presence might be; I later found out that although Thailand and Malaysia were on good terms, the latter kept a sharp eye on her border because the troubles of Thailand's neighbours had to some extent destabilised that country, and the Malaysians wanted to prevent any troublesome influences from affecting their own territory as well. We heard that the Communists were at work in Thailand and were particularly strong in the south.

After our passports had been checked at the Malaysian border post, the barrier was raised and we walked into the Land of Smiles. Things were more relaxed here. There was no military presence — just a policeman and a few officials at a wooden building with a tin roof which served as a customs post. As we filled in the various forms and talked with the officials, it became apparent to us that English was not as well known here as in the other Asian countries we had visited.

As we began to head north, we started to get an impression of what Thailand was like. To begin with, the country was densely forested, and just occasionally there would be a clearing with a few wooden houses and some land under cultivation. But as we travelled north, there were more villages and towns and open land. Thailand seemed to be poorer than Malaysia, and the rural people didn't look quite as well off as their counterparts on the other side of the border. However, the plains of Thailand were very fertile, and this asset, combined with high temperatures, plentiful rainfall and well-developed irrigation, enabled the country to be the world's second largest exporter of rice. The Thai people had plenty of food to eat and seemed to be in generally good health. So while Thailand was not as prosperous as Singapore and Malaysia, it was in an entirely different league from the impoverished states of the Indian subcontinent.

Hat Yai, where we spent our first night in Thailand, was a bustling town with a modern commercial centre, big shops, luxurious hotels and a thriving night life. Great crowds roamed the streets in the evening — many of them young people wearing T-shirts and blue jeans — eating and drinking in the restaurants, shopping and trading and visiting the cinemas and night-clubs, while the ladies of the night plied their age-old trade.

Hat Yai was also a centre of tourism, and so, after spending the night in the cheapest Chinese hotel we could find, we went to the tourist office to ask if it was safe to cycle in Thailand. Since arriving in the country, I had been feeling distinctly uneasy, as if passing through an evil and hostile environment. We had heard frightening stories of people being robbed and even murdered in Thailand, and even some Thai people had warned us to be careful, saying, 'Some bad people here could be smiling in your face and sticking a knife in your back at the same time!' At the tourist office I spoke with a very attractive Thai girl and explained my fears. She smiled charmingly and said, 'The stories you hear are only a few little incidents, but the newspapers make a big shout about them. No, it is very safe in Thailand. No problem!'

I wasn't convinced by her assurances, but we decided to press on regardless. We considered continuing our journey by train, but I felt that would have displayed a lack of faith in God, who had protected and guided us all the way so far. So we got on our bikes and took the road from Hat Yai which ran up the east coast of the peninsula, beside the western limit of the Gulf of Thailand. Once again we were travelling by the back roads, avoiding the main north-south highway which ran along the west coast.

The road was well surfaced, and that factor, together with the cooling effect of the sea breezes, meant that we made very good progress. There was plenty of other traffic on the road too, including buses, trucks, Japanese cars and, surprisingly, quite a number of big, cumbersome, petrol-guzzling American cars. There were also a great many motorbikes. Apparently most Thai rural families own one of these rather than a car. We were greatly amused by one sight we saw: a small, thin Thai man driving a motorbike, with three large Thai women squeezed on to the back of it. However, the bike wasn't finding the experience in the least bit amusing, and its engine was making a harsh, choking noise and exuding clouds of oily, black smoke. A little further on we saw a man riding a bicycle, with two monkeys for company. And as if that weren't enough, we saw two cows among the passengers of a bus! It was all part of a day's cycling in Thailand.

Our first night on the coast was spent in a very small town called Sathing Phra. When we arrived, we discovered that there was no hotel there. However, we soon located the local English teacher, who introduced us to a friend who invited us to stay the night in his wooden house. In the evening, they took us out for a meal at the local eating-house and then brought us to the town's Buddhist temple, where the Buddha's birthday was being celebrated. Situated within a walled compound which was entered through an arched gateway, it was about the size of a British detatched house and had a very steep roof made of red tiles. Beneath the roof were white walls and pillars embellished with gold paint. In another part of the compound was the pagoda: a large, grey, bell-shaped monument.

There was a bright, full moon and the atmosphere seemed a little eerie to me. I felt tense and out of place, afraid that John and I would be seen as evil Westerners. I feared that we might even be attacked. However, I was soon put at ease by the warm friendliness of the people, and I relaxed when I realised that nothing sinister was going to happen. A priest, sitting cross-legged on the steps of the pagoda, simply gave a talk, and then the orange-robed, head-shaven monks and the rest of the worshippers paraded around it, carrying lights. The people then stood around in groups chatting, and the whole event turned into something of a social occasion.

After the ceremony, I could not help but reflect on

the disparity between the beliefs and behaviour of the Thai people. Buddhism advocated a life of peace and meditation, and yet ironically this, the only Buddhist country we were to pass through on our trip around the world, also happened to be the most violent. There had to be something wrong: somehow the people's beliefs just didn't get translated into their everyday lives. It occurred to me that this was because the only way to find true peace is to be at peace with God through Jesus Christ. In order to have a peaceful society, the Thais needed to repent of their wrong actions and motives, allow Jesus to save them from sin and death and make him the Lord of their lives. Only when he was in control, would they be able to live peacefully with one another.

The next day we continued our trek along the coast, occasionally stopping by the sea to watch the fishing boats and to enjoy the cool breezes. A swim in the waters of the Gulf would have been very welcome, but bathing was dangerous there because of the large numbers of jellyfish, so we had to content ourselves with the extremely refreshing ice-cold sugar-cane drinks which we could buy along the road.

Once when we were resting under a coconut tree, looking out on the sea, a local man came along and greeted us and, using a sharp knife on the end of a long pole, cut down a coconut for each of us. Then, using a cleaver, he cut them open so that we could drink the cool, refreshing milk and eat the white kernel. We were very touched by this act of kindness towards two foreign travellers.

We encountered many similar friendly gestures on our journey through Thailand. As we cycled along, many of the people smiled or waved at us and the children would laugh and giggle. The older people were somewhat shy with us, but the younger men would often shout, 'Hey you!' at us as we passed by. We frequently heard this dozens of times in an hour, and so it became rather tiresome. It was also a little intimidating, as we got the impression that these shouts of greeting were not altogether friendly. (However, some missionaries we met in Thailand later assured us that it was indeed an amicable gesture.) I continued to feel uneasy in Thailand, and I was not reassured when I heard that recently a missionary had been shot in the head while preaching on the street or when a cyclist from New Zealand whom we met told us he had been robbed in Thailand the previous year.

We were sure that the intentions of some of the people who spoke to us were dubious. On one occasion, two men in a Toyota pick-up truck pulled alongside us as we were cycling and started asking questions like 'Where do you come?' 'Where do you go?' 'Where do you stay last night?' I gave them only the briefest of answers, unwilling to tell them very much. They drove beside me for a while, and as they talked among themselves, I prayed that God would keep plenty of traffic coming, so that they wouldn't dare to do anything criminal. Eventually they drove off without saying good-bye, and later we passed them as they were sitting at the roadside. They shouted aggressively as John and I cycled past, but we kept going, praying all the while. Later, as we arrived at a seaside town where we planned to stay the night, we saw them again. They glared at us sullenly, but we saw no more of them.

On another occasion, a young man came alongside me on his bicycle and made a gun-at-the-head gesture at me, but I'm not sure if this was meant as a threat or a warning. Whatever the intention was, the incident sent shivers down my spine.

Praying constantly for protection, we continued on our way up the east coast. On our journey we heard many other stories of Thai violence. Recently vicious

Thai fishermen had boarded crowded junks carrying Vietnamese boat people, who in desperation had fled oppression in their own country and were seeking a new home. The Thais plundered whatever valuables they could find, killed many of the men and raped the women and girls. Violence seemed to be a disease in the very soul of Thailand.

On 18th May, after two weeks of cycling in Thailand, we arrived at the capital, Bangkok. It was a noisy, crowded, sprawling city afflicted with chronic traffic congestion, and was a mixture of the modern and the ancient, of the smart and sophisticated and the grubby and dilapidated. Some of the shops were just simple little cubicles opening on to the street, while others were plush, modern, air-conditioned retail outlets for the big names like Sony, Ford and Hoover. Then there were the labyrinthine market areas, which were usually roofed over because of the heavy monsoon rains. In the centre of the city were many smart, new office blocks, hotels and public buildings, and there were Buddhist temples everywhere. Many of the people were well dressed and looked prosperous, and they were usually very willing to smile, be helpful and attempt to sell one something!

While in Bangkok, we stayed with Frank and Helen Kalf, whose names had been given to us back home in Ireland. Frank was a Dutchman who was employed by the United Nations Food and Agriculture Organisation, while Helen came from Northern Ireland and was very involved in the activities of the churches in the city. During our stay she took us to a local prison, where we distributed clothes, books and magazines on behalf of the International Church in Bangkok among the illegal Burmese immigrants there.

Frank and Helen lived in a complex of private houses which had its own indoor swimming pool and a guarded entrance. During our first evening with them I remarked,

'You've certainly got plenty of security around here, haven't you? When we arrived, the man at the gate didn't want to let us in!'

'Yes,' said Helen, 'I'm afraid Bangkok is a dangerous place to live in. A lot of robberies take place here, and Westerners are particularly at risk because they're comparatively rich.'

'Yes, nearly everyone we meet tells us about the robberies,' agreed John. 'It seems that most people here have either been robbed or know someone who has been.'

'We've been told some horrible stories about the crimes that go on here,' I added. 'We heard of one incident where someone's finger was cut off for the sake of a ring!'

'Oh yes, and even worse things than that can happen!' said Helen. 'You need to be very careful here. Don't walk about showing anything valuable like a camera.'

'What do you think is the reason for all this crime and violence?' asked John.

'Well, the troubles in the neighbouring countries have a lot to do with it,' replied Frank, 'but personally I wonder if Buddhism isn't also to blame in some way. You see, the people are taught from childhood that they shouldn't show anger, or any emotion at all for that matter. The result is that their repressed emotions build up inside them until the pressure causes some sort of outburst — often violent. That's what I think, anyway.'

'If you should happen to run into any trouble — and we pray you don't, of course — the best thing you can do is to give no resistance to the robbers. Let them take what they want. If you do resist them, they might get violent.'

These were sobering thoughts, and they cast a shadow of anxiety over our time in Thailand.

One very depressing aspect of what we saw of life in

Bangkok was the widespread prostitution and pornography. There seemed to be pornographic cinemas and theatres everywhere, and on the streets great numbers of very young Thai girls flaunted their bodies. One man approached me and offered to show me some pictures of girls who were for hire — some of them were only thirteen, he said. It saddened me deeply to think that those girls were so poor that they had no choice but to degrade themselves just to stay alive. It made me sad, too, to think that while God had designed sex to be a beautiful way of expressing love within the context of marriage, those girls knew it only as a desperate, sordid means of making a meagre living. It seems that the world over, depraved humanity takes God's precious gifts and debases them.

We spent some time seeing the sights of the city, visiting a number of temples and travelling on the river-buses which used the Chao Phraya River and its many canals as thoroughfares. We also took a day trip along the 'Death Railway' to see the famous bridge over the River Kwai and the Kanchanaburi War Cemetery, where 6,000 Allied prisoners of war who had died building the railway were buried.

While we were in Bangkok, we made arrangements for our travel to the USA. Thai International Airways offered us a flight to Seattle for the equivalent of just £225 each, which was unbeatable value. However, because luggage was costed on size, the price they quoted for our bikes was totally out of the question. For a while, it looked as if we might have to leave them behind us when we left Thailand, but once again we asked God to intervene in a tricky situation. Then I went back to the booking office and spoke to two very helpful Thai ticket girls. They rang the airport and discovered that a special low price was supposed to be charged for bikes, so our problem was solved. However, as it turned out, in the end we didn't have to pay anything for the bikes at the airport, because the official concerned couldn't be bothered with the paper work!

We had spent a very pleasant and interesting few days in Bangkok, but we were now eager to move on in order to see the Tear Fund refugee camp. Over the weekend we stayed at the Overseas Missionary Fellowship hospital at Manoram, a town just to the north of the capital, and on Monday 24th May we set out on the 106-mile journey to Kamphaeng Phet, our next port of call. Despite the high temperature and the overhead sun, we were amazed to find that we were able to maintain speeds of twenty miles per hour for hours on end.

Towards the end of the day, as we were cycling down a long, empty stretch of road, I heard a small motorbike approaching from the rear. I glanced round and saw that there were three young men on the bike and that they were pulling up beside John, who was about fifteen yards behind me. Then the men started shouting at John, and I glanced round again in alarm. I was horrified by what I saw. One of the men was wielding a large-bore hand-gun!

'Oh no! Not that!' I said to myself in shock. 'Anything but that!' I braked to a dead stop. 'Lord, please don't let them harm John!' I prayed.

Paralysed by fear, I watched the ugly situation which was developing. John had stopped too, now about twenty yards behind me. Two of the young men jumped off the bike as the third one turned it around. The one with the gun waved it at John, indicating that he should hold his hands up, while the other one set about cutting the bags off his bike. I realised it would be foolish of me to try to intervene, because I might make the robbers panic and shoot, or they might just rob me too. 'Lord, don't let John try to stop them,' I prayed. 'Just let them get what they want!'

I was just wondering whether I would also be robbed when a stream of traffic came down the road, and this scared the men off. Hurriedly they jumped on their motorbike and accelerated away in a trail of smoke, taking two of John's bags with them. I waved to the passing cars and pointed to the motorbike as it sped away, hoping someone would stop, but no one wanted to get involved. There were some people in a nearby field tending their buffaloes. I shouted to them, 'Robbery! Robbery! Police! Police!' but got no response. They must have seen this sort of thing going on all the time.

I walked back up the road to console John. He had been badly shaken by the incident and had gone very pale. However, after a drink of water and a short rest we continued on our way — there was nothing else we could do. But we were afraid — afraid the robbers would come back. Each motorbike which passed by now terrified us.

As we cycled along and I mulled over what had happened, I realised I had received my first big jolt of the whole trip. I knew God promised to be with those who put their faith in him, so how could he have allowed John to be robbed and threatened with violence? I felt let down.

But later, when John reminded me that as well as containing his short-wave radio, cameras, passport, sleeping bag and personal effects, the two bags the robbers had stolen had also held a large quantity of Thai gospel tracts that had been given to us a few weeks earlier, I felt a lot better about it all. Perhaps God had allowed John's things to be stolen just so that those tracts could get into the hands of people who desperately needed to read them. All our possessions were really God's possessions, so who were we to argue with that?

Also, I realised that we had a lot to be thankful for, because although the robbery could so easily have involved violence, no harm had come to us.

Later that day we reached Kamphaeng Phet, where we met two missionaries — a New Zealander named John and a South African named Dave — both of whom were working with WEC International there. When they heard our story, they dropped what they were doing and took us to the local police station, where they translated our Northern Irish English into the Thai language. The police were very helpful, although their typically Thai tendency to smile and even laugh seemed rather out of place as we related what had happened to us.

John and I had the second nasty shock of our day as we were being driven back to the scene of the crime in a police pick-up truck. Up ahead in the darkness we could see flames and flashing lights and a lot of people standing around. Obviously there had been an accident. As we got nearer, we passed some burning tyres which had been put by the roadside as a hazard warning. A big, south-bound truck was standing on the wrong side of the road, its front dented. Its lights were the ones which we had seen flashing from the distance. Smashed into the front of the truck was a tangle of metal which had once been a taxi. Our police car was the first on the scene, so we had to stop. The two policemen got out to investigate the accident. We jumped out too and stood with the rest of the bystanders, watching the scene of gory carnage which was illuminated by the dancing red-and-yellow light from the burning tyres. The unfortunate taxi driver was hanging limply out of the driver's door, his lifeless head on the ground and his legs torn by jagged metal. In the back seat someone was groaning and writhing with pain, lying across another body that was slumped and still. Worst of all, in the front passenger seat we could make out another victim — a bloody mess incarcerated in crushed metal beneath the bumper of the truck — someone who a few minutes ago had been a healthy, living person. Someone else was lying on the road behind the car. He appeared to be only slightly injured and was being attended to by those who had been first on the scene. The truck driver, himself unscathed, had evidently run away from the scene of the accident, afraid of being arrested and jailed.

It had indeed been a very sobering day — a day when death had stared us in the face twice. As I stood there looking on that scene of death and destruction and thinking what could have happened to John and me during the robbery, I reflected on just how sudden and unexpected death could be. It could strike at any moment. I was shocked by the day's events, but I was also challenged and moved — challenged to let God have the whole of my life and to be always ready to die, ready to meet my Maker with a clear conscience. And I was moved as I wondered about the spiritual state of the young men who had just died. Earlier that evening they had had their plans, hopes and dreams, just like anyone else, never for one moment suspecting that death lay just a little way ahead and would come without any warning.

That night the police had no time to investigate our robbery, so it was not until the next day that we returned to the scene of the crime. After telling them what had happened to us, we then had to return to Bangkok to see the British Consul, because of the loss of John's passport. A new one was issued to him, but while we were at the embassy, John's original passport was handed in by a Buddhist monk. Following the advice of the Consul, we regretfully gave up any notion of further cycling in Thailand. It was a great disappointment after eight and a half long months of strenuous cycling not to be able to arrive at the Sob Tuang Refugee Camp on our bikes.

On Saturday 29th May, after a twelve-hour bus journey through the night, we finally reached Maejarim Christian Clinic and the compound where its Tear Fund workers lived. The Clinic was situated on the outskirts of Maejarim, a small town about twenty-five miles from the provincial centre of Nan in the north-east of Thailand, near the border with Laos. We spent the next three days at the Clinic and at the nearby Sob Tuang Refugee Camp, seeing the work that Tear Fund was doing.

Since 1975, tribal groups from Laos had been crossing jungles, rivers and mountains in order to get to Thailand to avoid Communist oppression. According to some first-hand reports, the Communist forces had taken many tribal people away from their homes to camps for the purpose of 're-education' (in reality indoctrination), while many others had been killed and their villages ransacked. This persecution was carried out because some of the tribal groups were purported to have sided with the Americans during the Vietnam War. So many people had fled to Thailand, and thousands of them made it to the YMCA's Sob Tuang Refugee Camp.

At around the same time a similar exodus of refugees from Kampuchea had taken place, during that unfortunate country's bloody and devastating civil war. This exodus attracted world attention and so the response by international agencies was rapid, large-scale and well co-ordinated. However, the situation of the Laotian refugees was just as desperate, but it received far less publicity, with the result that the Sob Tuang Camp was underfunded and under-resourced. So it was against this background that Tear Fund were invited by the YMCA to take over much of the running of the Clinic and the Camp. Technically they were separate projects, but in practice they worked together closely.

The Clinic had in-patient accommodation for twenty people, an out-patient department, an opium detoxification ward, X-ray and laboratory equipment and a small operating theatre. These medical facilities served the people of Maejarim, who had no other local clinic. Also, mobile medical teams went out to four outlying villages twice a week. The Clinic also cared for seriously ill patients from the Refugee Camp.

The Camp was reached by travelling for three miles along a rocky, deeply rutted dirt road that wound its way up and around densely forested hills. Although it did not have a boundary fence, we had to pass through a security gate manned by the Thai authorities. The dwellings in the Camp, built by the refugees themselves out of bamboo and thatch, were scattered over several wooded hills, close to a river. So in many ways it resembled the villages which the tribal people had left behind. It provided refuge for four main ethnic groups: the Hmong (the largest), the Lao, the Htin and the Yao. Each group lived within its own village or *khet* within the Camp. Altogether it covered an area of about three-quarters of a square mile.

The only sanitation was pits dug in the earth, and the water supply, drawn from wells, was inadequate. Additional water had to be carried up from the muddy river in the valley below, since the only pump house had been flooded out some time ago when the river level rose by fifty feet during one night of heavy rain. However, although living conditions in the Camp were primitive, they were similar to those the people had been used to back in their own tribal lands.

Life in the Camp seemed to be going on as normal – or as near to normal as was possible in the circumstances. We saw one man rethatching his hut, another squatting on the ground, sharpening an axe against a stone. Another walked past us with a pet green parrot perched on his shoulder. The women were dressed in brightly coloured tribal clothes and were busy preparing food and looking after their children. Many of them were also involved in handicraft projects run by the relief agencies. The children, when they weren't attending the YMCA school, played football noisily and were very eager to be photographed. They smiled and laughed a great deal and seemed happy, blissfully ignorant of the insecurity of their people's situation. However, when I tried to photograph one little boy, he cried. I wondered if he had witnessed someone being shot back in Laos, and thought I was pointing a gun at him.

Although there were several other organisations working in the Camp in various capacities such as education and handicrafts, Tear Fund was the main agency, having responsibility for looking after the health and welfare of the people and also for seconding teachers to the Camp's YMCA school.

Dr Andrew Brown, Tear Fund's chief worker at Maejarim and Sob Tuang, showed us around the Camp's hospital, which was a hive of vital activity. It was composed of a twenty-two-bed ward, a small clinical laboratory and dispensary, two large out-patient clinics each catering for around 200 people every week, and also underfives, family-planning, antenatal and dental clinics. Another important feature of Tear Fund's health policy in the Camp was a community-health programme under the direction of Dr John Sayers, as a part of which a mobile morning clinic visited the Camp's *khets*.

All this work was, of course, too much for the three doctors to cope with alone, so the training of paramedical personnel — refugees themselves — was of crucial importance. They were taught how to deal with diseases common among the Camp population, such as malaria, cholera and typhoid.

Another important part of the health programme was opium detoxification, since addiction to the drug, which was very easily available in that part of the world, was very common. Patients were taken to the special ward at the Clinic in Maejarim, where withdrawal normally took about a month to achieve.

John and I came to the Camp expecting to find the people in a desperate condition. Instead, we found them well fed and in good health. But they were so well off only because of the work of Tear Fund and the other agencies. Conditions there were good compared with those in some of the other refugee camps in Thailand. In addition, through the witness of the Christian staff at the Camp, a number of the refugees had turned to Christ and had become members of the Camp's own church. Certainly, all those of us who contributed to the funding of the Camp can take satisfaction from the fact that we helped Tear Fund to tend the physical and spiritual needs of the refugees.

Even so, the situation of these people was far from ideal. To begin with, they were living in squalid conditions. Their dwellings were just small bamboo-and-thatch huts where perhaps as many as twenty people from three generations might live. Also, they were in a foreign land. They wanted to return to their homelands, and the Thai government and the United Nations also wanted them to be repatriated. But the people were afraid to go home to Laos because of the political climate there. So they remained at Sob Tuang, homesick yet fearful of going home. The Camp was no substitute for living in their own tribal lands and being able to pursue their traditional ethnic lifestyles. The people were not permitted to leave the Camp at will, and few of them enjoyed the dignity of being able to work. They had little control over their own lives, which were completely in the hands of the Thai government. To the authorities they were just statistics, and yet they were real people with real needs for security, self-respect and love. (Since that time Sob Tuang has closed; a few thousand refugees were sent to the West, but most — about 40,000 — were sent to another camp near the Laotian border.)

As I watched the healthy and well-fed children playing together in the Camp, just like happy youngsters anywhere else in the world, I thanked God for the relief agencies like Tear Fund which had contributed so much to their well-being. But I could not help but wonder anxiously what the future held for them. Where would they live once they were adults, and what quality of life could they hope to enjoy?

11

Across North America

After our stay at the Refugee Camp, we returned to Bangkok and caught our flight to the USA. As we sat in the Jumbo Jet while it waited on the runway for clearance to take off, we noticed a small plane approach and land within our field of vision. Our eyes lit up when we saw that it was a Shorts Skyvan, an aircraft built in Belfast. This was an encouraging reminder that after our time in the States, we would be on our way home.

So after over six months in the great continent of Asia, we left it and crossed the Pacific Ocean, passing from the Third World into the First. When we arrived in Seattle after our 8,000-mile journey, it was morning, so we were able to reassemble our bikes and do a day's cycling as soon as we arrived. We had to get to the north side of the city and find Barry and Debbie Ison, whose names had been given to us by someone in Dacca in Bangladesh. Seattle was a big, sprawling city and it took us all day to cross it from the airport on its southern edge. On the outskirts there were many fine houses, often built of white-painted wood. Then, further north there was a huge industrial area, parts of which looked badly run down. There were vast railway yards with dozens of tracks and many long goods trains. There were many grey, dreary tenement blocks. Compared to places like Germany and Switzerland, the city looked very untidy and scruffy, and there was a great deal of litter about. The roads were full of bumps and were generally in poor condition. I wondered if that was why American cars were so big and equipped with such powerful suspension.

We passed through the city centre, which had a lot of smart, tall, modern buildings and also some very neglected-looking areas. On the corners of the dingy streets groups of denim-clad young people stood about, apparently with nothing to do. Then we passed through another industrial area and then into the wealthy northern suburbs. There were many big houses and a plethora of golf clubs and restaurants. On the roads there were constant streams of big, expensive-looking cars. We passed by a marina where many luxurious cruisers and yachts were moored. The whole area was pleasantly green and leafy.

Our initial impression of America was that there seemed to be a prevailing atmosphere of optimism and freedom of choice. There was a great deal of wealth about and many of the people were doing very well for themselves. Although there were also some poor people, their poverty was by no means as abject as that of the poor in the Third World.

We stayed briefly with the Isons and then moved on to our next port of call, which was Vancouver in Canada. There we spent a very pleasant ten days with the Jennings family, who had originally come from Belfast. Vancouver was a big city with the sea on its west side and mountains to the north and east. It was generally less untidy and run down than Seattle and had many attractive parks. While we were there, we gave our bikes a thorough overhaul. Both were fitted with new bearings and cables and were cleaned down and oiled. My bike's rear wheel also needed some new spokes.

From Vancouver we set out eastwards, beginning our

long overland journey to New York, from where we would fly to Ireland. We planned to camp out most nights, because it was safe to do so in North America and because it would have been prohibitively expensive to stay in hotels. The cost of living was very much higher here than it had been in Asia. No longer would we be able to sit at a hawker's stall and buy a really filling meal for the equivalent of fifty pence! Back in India, a middle-class family would have owned a bicycle, while here they would have two cars and a pick-up truck. Frequently it amazed us that such incredible contrasts of wealth and poverty could exist on the same planet.

A few days out from Vancouver it started to rain, and carried on raining until mid-July. Not only did the rain make cycling unpleasant, but it also made camping difficult because the ground was always muddy. Despite the weather, we succeeded in making our way up the rugged Okanagan Valley to Vernon in British Columbia, a town set between the Cascades (the coastal mountain range) and the Rockies, that vast and beautiful chain of mountains which stretched for thousands of miles from Alaska to California. After Vernon we stayed in the mountains throughout July, and altogether travelled over 1,100 miles.

We were cycling through some of Canada's most magnificent national parks on our way towards the Great Continental Divide. The road was well surfaced and followed the river valleys, climbing progressively as we got further east. There were great forests everywhere, although in the valleys the trees had been cleared to make way for cattle and arable farming. We saw some extremely long trains winding their way through the valleys, with perhaps as many as five engines pulling literally hundreds of ore-carrying wagons. There were a great many lumber trucks on the roads, and holiday-makers in Dormobiles were also a common sight. The local Canadian people we saw generally looked healthy, prosperous and overweight.

We camped out most nights, but even that proved to be expensive. Sometimes we had to pay as much as eight dollars for one night at a campsite, and one proprietor asked us for eighteen dollars. We explained to him that we didn't want to buy the camp! Camping was great fun, although the persistent rain dampened our enthusiasm for it a little. It also dampened our sleeping-bags, clothes and tent, and it was nigh-on impossible to get them dried out, since it was raining so much of the time. However, as we moved south through the Rockies, the weather got warmer and there was plenty of sunshine instead of rain. The other major problem about camping was the ever-present mosquitoes. Some evenings there were so many of them that we just had to seal up our tent and go to sleep early!

The further east we travelled, the better were the views which we got of the majestic Rockies in the distance. Finally we reached them, and cycled up the Great Divide at Rogers Pass. It took a whole day's slogging in low gear, but our efforts were rewarded with an exhilarating free-wheel down the other side. The Great Divide is the watershed of North America, and at Kicking Horse Pass we saw the Divided Creek, from which some waters flow westwards into British Columbia and eventually end up in the Pacific Ocean, and other waters flow eastwards into Alberta and, thousands of miles further on, end up in the Atlantic Ocean. We were to cross the Great Divide twice more on our journey through the Rockies — at Vermilion Pass and at Flesher Pass.

And so we left Canada and returned to the United States, entering the state of Montana. We stayed the whole of the third week of July at Kalispell, a town in the west of the state, with Myron and Terri Swallow, two

American friends of mine. (I had met Myron when I was working among Christians in Eastern Europe, and we had done some trips over the Iron Curtain together.) That week proved to be one of the highlights of the whole trip around the world. The hard times we had endured in India were now behind us, our health was fully restored, our memories of the robbery in Thailand were fading, and we now enjoyed a whale of a time. We found ourselves on the receiving end of non-stop hospitality and while we were in Kalispell, did a multitude of enjoyable things, such as speed-boating on Flathead Lake, fishing for trout, white-water river rafting in Glacier International Peace Park and hiking across a snow-field. We also ate several sumptuous *smörgåsbord* meals (these went down particularly well with us, as we were allowed to eat as much as we possibly could for a fixed price!), attended church twice, went to some Bible classes on the creation/evolution debate and led a young people's meeting. Myron and Terri were very kind to us — as, indeed, were many people whom we met in Canada and the States. For example, after we left Kalispell, a Montana farmer and his wife invited us into their home for a typical American breakfast of pancakes and maple syrup and sent us away with four enormous steaks!

Quite a few of the people we ran into were of Irish ancestry and were very interested in the Emerald Isle. I had met a number of Irish Americans back home, and always got rather irritated when they disparagingly compared Ireland with the States. They would talk in glowing terms of the wealth, the open spaces, the tall, tall buildings, the amazing eight-lane freeways and the palatial homes. But, having seen the States for myself, I concluded that there was a lot of exaggeration in all that talk. The only tall buildings we saw were in the cities, and most of the American roads weren't a patch on Irish ones. In fact, they were among the worst on which we had to cycle during our trip around the world. They were often roughly surfaced, badly maintained and narrow. Because of their roughness, we were rarely able to cycle at maximum speed. Most of the roads linking the towns were paved, of course, but the majority of the minor roads were just gravel-and-dirt tracks. And even the freeways were disappointing. Many of them were just four-lane roads, with two lanes in each direction. Finally, most of the American houses we saw weren't all that palatial, and many of them were made of wood. Also, a lot of the people lived in mobile homes.

It took us a week to cycle the 430 miles from Kalispell to Yellowstone. The scenery became less dramatically mountainous as we reached the 7,000-foot-high plateau upon which the famous park was situated. As we entered it, we were a little worried by the signs we saw warning motorists to stay in their cars and keep their windows up as precautions against the many dangerous grizzly bears about. But what do you do if you're on a bicycle when a grizzly shows up? Cycle as fast as you can, presumably!

Yellowstone National Park (the world's first) gave us a very interesting start to August. It was a mixture of forest, moorland and big lakes. Its grasslands were adorned by hundreds of varieties of multicoloured wild flowers. There was all manner of fascinating wildlife about. We saw deer grazing, moose wandering beside the rivers and chipmunks scuttling about near the trees. Fortunately the bears kept out of our way! There was a great deal of geothermal activity in the region. We gathered with hundreds of other tourists to watch the world-famous geyser, Old Faithful, erupt right on time, throwing spray hundreds of feet into the air. We saw a small lake seething with sulphur gas, its waters spilling out over slimy, luridly coloured mud into a river. We saw pools of hot mud gurgling and bubbling, and we even went for a bathe in a warm, effervescent stream.

Until this time, the highest altitude we had attained had been back in Nepal, where we reached 8,199 feet. But now, in the first week of August, we climbed over three passes, all of which were higher than that. The first, Dunraven in Yellowstone, didn't present much difficulty; the second, Beartooth, at 10,947, was the highest of the whole trip, but wasn't a problem; but the last one, over the Bighorn Mountains, gave us real problems. The gradient was so steep that we had to get off our bikes and push them. Also, we happened to be there on an exceedingly hot day and this was a very dry, barren area with no water available for miles. We were relieved, to say the least, to reach the State Forest Campsite a quarter of the way up and quench our thirst there.

We passed through the state of Wyoming, staying at Sheridan, Gillette and Newcastle with some Christian contacts we had made, and then we pushed on through South Dakota. We passed by the famous Mount Rushmore, where the heads of Presidents Washington, Jefferson, Lincoln and Roosevelt had been carved into the side of a white cliff. They were an awesome sight, giant faces staring coldly at the horizon. We also passed through the region known as the Badlands, where ancient layered rock had been deeply eroded by the wind, leaving weird and fantastic pillars, buttes and gorges, some of them white, some striped red, orange and yellow. The area was almost totally lifeless, except for some sparse, yellow grass. It looked more like a landscape on the moon than one on earth.

We were now well out of the Rockies and among the gently rolling hills of the prairie. South Dakota seemed to consist mostly of huge wheat farms, and there were few trees. The roads were now better than they had been further west, and this factor, together with the terrain, enabled us to increase our daily mileage from around 60, which had been our average in the Rockies, to about 100. On 15th August we did our best day's cycling on the trip so far: 134 miles!

After South Dakota, we entered Minnesota. In the west of the state the country was flat prairieland, but as we cycled north-east towards Minneapolis, this gave way to more varied terrain. There were more trees now and the land was greener than South Dakota had been, where the golden hue of wheat had been the predominant colour. As cyclists weren't allowed to travel on the interstate roads in Minnesota, we had to take the smaller roads, which were narrow and very poorly surfaced. I had a miraculous escape from serious injury or death just south of Mankato, where a passing truck forced me off the road. My front wheel got stuck in the soft verge, causing my bike to slam to a halt. As a result, I was thrown off it right on to the middle of the road — a mere split-second after the last wheels of the enormous truck had passed by. Both the bike and I were slightly scratched, but otherwise in one piece. I thanked God for protecting me from harm yet again, and felt more assured than ever that he really was looking after us on our travels.

Another little miracle happened when we found that we were unable to stay with our contact in Minneapolis and as a result, were stranded in the middle of that metropolis of two million people in the late afternoon, many hours of cycling away from any campsites and unable to afford any accommodation in the city. We were at a loss as to where to go, and must have looked a pitiful sight standing at the roadside anxiously studying our maps. It just so happened that a native of Minneapolis named Tom Cresand passed by at that moment and asked us about our travels. When he understood our predicament, he said we were welcome to spend the night on the floor of his lounge. We slept very soundly on his deep-pile carpet! Tom was a keen cyclist himself and so was also able to tell us how to get through the city on pleasant, quiet roads, avoiding the busy thoroughfares.

After Minnesota, we entered Wisconsin. The roads there were also very bad, but it was a pleasant state to cycle through. The scenery was very varied, with many rivers, lakes, forests, big farms, little villages and towns. The land was displaying some of the reds and browns of the approaching autumn — a reminder that the summer had passed and that soon we would be home.

From Wisconsin we passed through Michigan and then left the USA again and entered Ontario. In the north it was rocky country, suitable only for rearing sheep, but as we drew closer to Toronto, the countryside became hilly and well cultivated. We were surprised to find that parts of the Trans Canadian Highway were only two lanes wide — one lane in each direction! There was a great deal of traffic and we were frequently pushed off the road by big, twenty-six-wheel lorries.

We had experienced great variety in the weather in August. Back on the Yellowstone Plateau the days had been pleasantly warm, and out on the prairies the weather had been mild and windy. In Minnesota, it had been hot and humid, and cold and wet in Michigan and Ontario. In fact, we were amazed one night in Ontario when the temperature fell to just thirty-six degrees Fahrenheit!

We ended the month in Toronto, the capital of Ontario. It was a beautiful city in a beautiful location, on the shores of Lake Ontario. It had many tall, modern buildings, but these did not make the city ugly, as they did in so many other places.

After Toronto, we passed back into the USA once more, seeing as many sights as we possibly could on the way. We stopped off at Niagara Falls, and found them to be every bit as impressive as we had expected. We arrived in the evening in darkness, and we could hear the roar and rumble of the falling water from a long way off. The next day we stood for a long time watching the water rushing down over the Falls. At the foot of the Falls were boats carrying tourists which deliberately got as close as possible to the thunderous deluge. Sometimes the boats completely disappeared as great clouds of spray obscured them from view. Later we donned caps and capes and had a ride in a lift which took us down the face of the falls, with the water cascading in front of us. It was a frightening but also exhilarating way of appreciating the awesome power of God's creation.

We stopped off at New York and visited the Empire State Building, the World Trade Centre, the United Nations Headquarters and the Statue of Liberty. New York was a very impressive place with its skyscrapers, bright lights and big stores, but there was another side to it as well. The roads were in very bad condition and there were many scruffy, run-down areas of dirty tenement blocks. There were a lot of poor people about, some of them looking very tough and aggressive. One of my most lasting impressions of the place is the fear I had of being attacked or mugged. New York's underground railway was a very frightening place to be, particularly at night. On one occasion, while we were crossing under the Hudson River, a man ran in from the next carriage, shouting that there was a fight going on there.

Washington DC was a different sort of place altogether. It had an air of grandeur about it, and I felt thrilled to be in the capital of the most powerful country in the world. While we were there, we of course visited the Capitol building and the White House.

Our journey through North America had given me plenty of food for thought. The wealth we had seen had come as something of a shock to us after the poverty of Asia. Here we had seen families going off on holiday in enormous Dormobiles, some of them as large as buses and equipped with colour television, air-conditioning and every conceivable luxury, with a small car for use on short trips on tow. Those Dormobiles, which were used for just a few weeks in the year, were far better in every respect than the permanent homes of Asia's poor.

A thought which really bothered me was that many of the rich people in North America and the West as a whole were Christians, and read the same Bible as their fellow believers whom we had met in the Orient. Western Christians understand that salvation is a free gift from God and that nothing they can do can earn it. But some seem to forget that having received that salvation, they must then yield themselves to God as living sacrifices. Jesus is our Lord, and all that we are and all the material things that we own should be at his disposal. But instead of seeking first his kingdom and his righteousness and laying up treasures in heaven, many Christians are accumulating wealth for their temporary stay here on earth. While Western Christians pamper themselves with luxuries, their brothers and sisters in the developing countries are going hungry and their children are dying of easily preventable diseases.

The people of North America were often very kind to us, sometimes buying us meals or sending us away loaded up with food. While we greatly appreciated their generosity, it has to be said that they were giving from their plenty. By contrast, the poor people we had met in Pakistan and India had given just as generously out of a situation of poverty. Some of the Christians we met in Asia would have killed their last chicken in order to give us a good meal, and those people in the Christian village in Pakistan had been eager to give us money for the refugees in Thailand when they desperately needed the cash themselves to pay for the medical treatment of their sick children. Their truly sacrificial giving spoke to me powerfully about what it means to really be a servant of Jesus Christ, what it really means to love God and our neighbours as ourselves. If the rich Christians gave as sacrificially as this and demonstrated God's love in such practical ways, the church would make a far greater impact upon the world.

Another thought which occurred to me about North America was that religion was important to most of the people there, just as it had been in Asia. It struck me with renewed clarity that whether people are rich or poor, they still search for meaning in life and for spiritual reality.

In Thailand, I had been scared by the violence there and blamed Buddhism for it. And yet a so-called Christian country like the USA was just as violent, if not more so. I wondered if this was because most people in America were only nominal Christians and had never personally experienced the risen Jesus Christ for themselves, and so were left untouched by his love and power. Or was America a violent place because the church was so vibrant there, and the forces of evil were doing their utmost to counteract the good influence of the gospel? These were tough questions, and I didn't have all the answers.

It was with a feeling of pride and excitement that on Tuesday 13th September we boarded the Aer Lingus Jumbo Jet which would take us from Kennedy Airport at New York to Shannon. As we left New York and the great continent of North America far below us and headed out over the Atlantic, I felt sorry to be coming to the end of our round-the-world trip, which had been such a wonderful experience in many ways. But I was also keen to get home to be with my family and friends.

12
A Time to Reflect

As our Jumbo Jet began to lose altitude and passed over the misty Irish coast at dawn on Wednesday morning, I felt overjoyed that after our round-the-world journey we had made it safely home. I vividly remembered sailing down Belfast Lough on our way to England a year ago, wondering whether we would ever see home again — and here we were! I gave thanks to God for guiding and protecting us throughout the year.

John's parents met us at Shannon airport and accompanied us in their car as we cycled north on the very last leg of our journey. It was a real pleasure to once again be in the quiet, Irish countryside, where the roads were so good and the drivers were courteous and considerate to cyclists. Later we met up with my parents and family. It was such a joy and a relief to be with them again after such a long separation.

As we crossed the border into Northern Ireland the next day, we were delighted to pass through the towns and villages that we knew so well. Near Dungannon we were joined by dozens of supporters who had come to cycle the last few miles with us. As we passed through the villages of Castlecaulfield and Donaghmore, people waved to us and clapped. Along the road near my home someone held aloft a banner reading, 'Welcome home,

2 Johns'. We came into the town centre at the head of a cavalcade of bell-ringing cyclists to be greeted by a civic reception in the Market Square. A crowd of about 2,000 cheering people had gathered to welcome us home. The Dungannon Silver Band were playing 'When the Saints Go Marching In'. I felt a great sense of achievement as we finally stopped our bikes and got off. People all around us were clapping and slapping us on the back. It was a very moving moment for us both.

We went up on to the platform that had been erected for the occasion in the Square. Welcoming speeches made by Ralph Brown, the chairman of Dungannon District Council, by the Very Revd Dr David Burke of the Presbyterian Church of Ireland and by Graham Fairbairn of Tear Fund. Mr Brown remarked that he couldn't believe that a whole year had passed since we had last stood in this same square at the start of our journey. Neither could we! Dr Burke said our trip was 'an adventure inspired by the Spirit of God. He started with them, he went through it all with them. The glory is to God and to his kingdom and his work.' Graham Fairbairn said the past year would be one John and I would never forget. 'I pray that the rest of us may also never forget it and the challenge it has brought to us,' he said.

After that, John and I were kept busy for a long time, signing autographs for the scores of young people who had crowded around us. The climax to the civic reception was in the Scotch Street Halls in the town, where tea was served and the people had a chance to talk to us. It was a wonderful home-coming, and we felt deeply moved and touched by the enthusiasm of the welcome we received.

In countless ways during our trip, God had shown that he was in charge of the whole thing. Time and again, events made us feel that the trip was being run by an authority higher than ourselves. It would be true to say that the whole trip worked like clockwork from start to finish, but I wouldn't say that we were lucky. Our trip went well because of prayer.

At the start of every day on our travels we prayed, admitting our weakness and our need of God's guidance and protection. It was also a very important source of encouragement for us to know that back home our families and friends were praying for us, and we had no doubt that those prayers were helping us in very tangible ways. God made use of the physical and mental resources which we possessed, but many times we asked him to intervene when our resources were exhausted, and he faithfully responded to our prayers. Often in Europe, Asia and North America we found ourselves without a place in which to spend the night. So we would pray, and it was fascinating to see how circumstances would suddenly change and a safe place to sleep would be provided for us. My managing to obtain that sprocket-block at Ludhiana, the only place in India where it could be obtained, and just a few days before I needed it, was too unlikely to be a mere coincidence!

These were the types of occurrences which I had read about in Christian books, but before the trip I hadn't really experienced them for myself. It was so encouraging to discover that God answered the prayers of an ordinary person like me! Even though the robbery in Thailand shook me, there was a positive side to it, because neither of us was harmed — and people were often killed in such incidents — and I like to think that those Thai tracts which the robbers inadvertently took away with them had a good effect. Who knows — perhaps a new church exists in Thailand right now because we were robbed that day! So throughout our travels, God proved to us in very practical ways that he was real and that he cared about our well-being, and as the months passed, we grew increasingly aware of this.

God had blessed the whole trip, and he continued to bless us afterwards too. One thing our parents had been concerned about was our finding employment once we came home. Within weeks of getting back, John was offered a job as a sales representative which was better than the one he had given up. During the civic reception, I chatted with Graham Fairbairn and told him that I was looking for a job for the next year, and that I needed to have flexible working hours so that I could visit and talk to all the support groups, schools, youth groups and churches which had been interested in the trip. I was prepared to do any sort of job in order to be able to do this vital follow-up work. It just so happened that Tear Fund had recently appointed a new Regional Organiser in Ireland, since Graham had changed jobs and become the organisation's Director of Public Services, but the appointee was unable to take up the position for at least six months. And so it was that a month after coming home I started work as a temporary Regional Organiser, and was thus able to combine my paid work with all the visiting I needed to do. Once again, God proved to us that he is a loving heavenly Father who is eager to provide all of our needs.

The first aim of our trip around the world had been to bring the reality of poverty in the Third World to the attention of the people of Northern Ireland. I believe it was successful in this. The project had a strong appeal to local people, principally because the two cyclists were from Northern Ireland. Our departure and return had received extensive media coverage. Ulster Television carried the story of our departure on their *Good Evening Ulster* programme and BBC Television's *Scene Around Six* took a lot of trouble interviewing us in a studio when we left and 'on location' outside Dungannon on our return. We had many interviews on local radio, being featured on the *Good Morning Ulster* news programme, the Sunday religious affairs programme, *Sunday Sequence*, and Walter Love's chat show, *Day by Day*. All the provincial newspapers told the story of our travels and our local newspaper, *The Tyrone Courier*, published monthly accounts of our adventures together with a selection of photographs. On our return, a number of national Christian magazines carried extensive stories about the trip.

We had also got a certain amount of media coverage in the countries through which we travelled. For example, as we passed through one town in Pakistan, a local newspaper reporter, interested by our unusual and heavily laden bicycles, followed us on his motorbike and interviewed us for his paper as we were cycling along! While I was recovering from malaria in India, two reporters and a photographer interviewed me at length. We heard from a missionary a year later that those photos, as well as being printed in India, had appeared in at least one newspaper in Japan. In all these instances, the interviewers tended to be most interested in our route, bikes and experiences, but they also enquired into our motives for undertaking the trip, so this gave us an opportunity to explain that we were trying to draw attention to Third World poverty because we were Christians.

The second aim of the trip had been to raise money in Northern Ireland for Tear Fund's work among the refugees in Thailand. Our committee had worked tirelessly while we were away, soliciting financial support and passing on information about our latest adventures to support groups. We were sponsored in quite a number of different ways, but one of the most popular was to give according to the distance we cycled. Even if someone sponsored us for only a penny per mile, over

13,000 miles of cycling brought the total to £130. Other fund-raising activities included jumble-sales, monthly bread-and-cheese lunches, gospel concerts and the sale of souvenir tea-towels. A large part of the sponsorship came from the Dungannon district, but the project was also supported by youth groups all over Northern Ireland. In fact, the largest amount raised by a single group came from the Malone Crusaders in Belfast. By the end of the year-long trip, a total of £25,000 had been raised, and during the two years of fund-raising which followed, that figure rose to £53,960. After that even more money came in, but we stopped counting! Every penny of this sum went directly to Tear Fund for their work in Thailand, since the funds for the costs of the trip had been raised separately.

The third and final aim of the venture had been to encourage Christians to see and fulfil their responsibilities to those in need around the world. This aim was fulfilled after the trip, when John and I visited the dozens of supporting groups, showing slides of our travels and communicating the reality of Third World poverty. We would always try to make clear to people the biblical basis to the trip, that is, that God cares about people's physical needs as well as their spiritual ones. This concern is clearly expressed in both the Old and New Testaments. In the Old Testament we see that God was always concerned about spiritual matters — righteousness, obedience and repentance — but he also showed his concern for those who were in physical need, and gave laws to help those who were not able to fend for themselves. In the New Testament, it is clear that Jesus came first and foremost to save the lost and to bring sinners to repentance and into a right relationship with God, but it is also very obvious that he cared about the hungry, the sick and anyone in physical distress. He said that the most important commandment in the Law was to 'love the Lord your God with all your heart and with all your soul and with all your mind and with all your strength,' but he also said that the second most important one was to 'love your neighbour as yourself' (Mt 22:37–9; Mk 12:30–1). He was saying that love for God and love for one's fellow man cannot be separated; if we claim to love God, we must also love people and be concerned for their well-being. So while the Bible clearly teaches that salvation is a free gift from God and cannot be earned by good works, it also makes it equally clear that good works are to be expected from the person who has been born again through Christ. These works should be the Christian's grateful response to God for saving him and giving him new life.

Through the many slide presentations we made in the year following the trip, we tried to convey the truth that the Christian, having been bought from sin and death by God through the sacrifice of his only Son, is no longer his own but is God's property. Christians need to acknowledge Jesus not only as their Saviour but also as their Lord, the One who is in command of their lives. God today is still the same God who in the Bible expressed his concern for the poor and the vulnerable, so he wants to go on expressing that concern through people who have yielded their lives to him and will do his will faithfully and selflessly. God wants to use our lives and everything that we are and own as channels through which his love can flow into the world.

Jesus said, 'I have come that they may have life, and have it to the full' (Jn 10:10). In order to enjoy this fullness of life, we must first gain peace with God by repenting of our sins and sinfulness, asking Christ to cleanse us by his blood and asking the Holy Spirit to indwell us and control us, so that our lives may be lived not for ourselves but for God and for other people. Another essential aspect of this fullness of life is the ability to enjoy the goodness of God's creation — to have decent health, clothing, food and housing. However, there are many people in the Third World who are Christians, who are in a right relationship with God and are serving him and others, but who are unable to enjoy real fullness of life because they lack the physical resources to do so: they are hungry, out of work, poorly housed and sick. The children of Christian parents die of malnutrition just as readily as those of non-Christian parents. Christians can die from diarrhoea and dehydration just like anyone else. So there is a great need for those Christians who have the material means to enjoy the fullness of life to share it with their brothers and sisters who do not.

And yet this is all before we even start to think about sharing the goodness of God with the non-Christian world. How on earth can a poverty-stricken Pakistani or Indian farmer see the love of God in rich Christians who have so much money that they don't even know how to spend it, and yet are reluctant to share it with those who are poorer? If people are to believe by what we say about Christ, they must also be convinced by the way we live.

Some Christians have emphasised the need for social action and the importance of alleviating physical suffering. In itself this emphasis is, of course, quite valid, but it is a mistake to think that this is all that Christianity is about. A priority of even greater importance is addressing people's need for spiritual salvation, without which they can have no relationship with God and ultimately can have no hope in life. However, other Christians, while very correctly emphasising that spiritual salvation is the top priority, have often completely overlooked the necessity of tending to people's physical needs. They have been concerned for their souls while seemingly having little concern for whether or not they have enough to eat. We Christians need to actually live the

Christian life, as this is the true test of whether or not someone has really become a Christian.

Today, as I look back on this trip of a lifetime, I do so with great thankfulness for the opportunity that I had, and I am glad that I took it. The whole journey was a wonderful experience in many ways. I learned so much about God and how real he is to real individuals in real situations. And I learned so much about the world and its people.

There were many highlights: the Christian village in Pakistan, the mighty Himalayan Mountains, the visit to the Sob Tuang Refugee Camp in Thailand, cycling across America from coast to coast. But I find that my strongest memories of the whole trip are of those children sleeping on the streets of the cities of India — some using flattened cardboard boxes as beds, others sprawled naked on the bare paving-stones, mere inches away from gutters overflowing with filth. Often as I'm going to sleep at night, I relive those experiences and wonder if I really do put God first in my life and if I love those children as much as I love myself. Jesus said, 'Whatever you did not do for one of the least of these, you did not do for me' (Mt 25:45). I wonder if I have really taken those words to heart.

Postscript

After the round-the-world trip, John's sense of calling to full-time Christian work continued to grow and develop. He was the Assistant Minister at First Lisburn Presbyterian Church from September 1985 until April 1988. He married in 1986 and obtained a BD degree. He and his wife Rosemary went for a few months to St Andrew's Hall Missionary College in Selly Oak, Birmingham, to attend a missionary training course.

On 1st October 1988 they went to Malawi in Africa, where until recently they were serving as missionaries in the city of Mzuzu in the north of the country. John was chaplain to the students in the schools and colleges. For health reasons they have now had to return to Ireland, where John is Minister of two Presbyterian churches.